Image this page 'Serenade Whisper' grown from seed 2021

Cultivating Curiosity

Growing Your Own Unique Dahlias from Seed

Written, Photographed & Designed by
Rebecca McConnell

Explore

Cultivating Your Curiosity

Growing and nurturing plants is one of life's simple joys. Gardening helps us transcend the distractions of a busy mind, and can effortlessly place us in a flow state of mental clarity. The astonishment felt when a tiny seed germinates, or when a cutting strikes can feel miraculous. And the beauty of a bloom like a dahlia, like art or music, touches us in a way which can be beyond words.

Furthermore, the full circle process of cultivating and nurturing plants through to maturity, and the inevitability of letting go at end of season, deepens our acceptance of the impermanence of life.

Imagine, then, the sheer delight for being responsible for a brand new dahlia coming into existence. Stewarding a dahlia bloom unlike any other, that has a distinct genetic code, and that has never existed anywhere else. Unlike most other flowers, this is what happens when you collect and grow dahlia seed. In this book, I'll explain not only why this is, but how you can participate in and artfully guide this natural process.

In the typical hustle bustle of our modern life, there is immeasurable benefit in slowing down and being present, and in spending time with nature. Paying attention to something as simple as a dahlia flower not only gets us out of our heads, but allows us to pay close attention to the minutiae and the details of natural beauty. Out of the seeming chaos of blending two remarkably complex genetic codes, we can learn to observe, and to lean into the unknowing and surrender to possibility. You will encounter a recurring theme throughout this book, that of finding your own way, just as each new dahlia seedling does.

Define your own goals, set your own assessment criteria, and do things to suit your own workflow and goals. I will give cues and suggest options, and offer insight to the way that works for me, but in every garden with its own idiosyncrasies, you need to learn to pay attention and make your own choices. Take time to slow down and observe and indulge your curiosity.

I will relate my own dahlia growing story in the final chapter of this book, but I'm certainly not alone in having found dahlias to be an extra special plant to grow. Whatever your knowledge or experience level in growing dahlias, I hope as you read through the pages of this book, and try your hand at growing them from seed, that you discover an even deeper appreciation for how unique dahlias are, and the extraordinary variations that are possible in their blooms. And as your understanding and ability to observe the nuance between each new dahlia grows, I do hope you find that it does indeed cultivate your curiosity even further.

Dahlia Diversity in the Genes

Dahlias are unique among flowers in their endless diversity of colour, size and form. A testament to nature's boundless creativity, there is a dahlia for every personal style and taste. Dahlias range from big blousy, open-petalled decorative types, to tiny perfect pompons with their intricate swirling petals that create natural fractals. Our brains respond to these geometric proportions even without consciously being aware of them.

With all the variation possible with dahlias, they satisfy our human desire to balance the familiar with new exciting stimuli that excites us.

How does one genus of flower give so many different looking blooms? The immense variation can be attributed to their octoploidal genetic structure - with 8 sets of chromosomes instead of the typical 2 sets in diploids (as found in most flowers, and even humans). When two dahlias cross to create seed, a complex blend of genes contribute to each characteristic, whether it be colour, size, petal arrangement. We will certainly explore each of these, as well as others, in more depth later.

The delightful thing is that even with very little scientific understanding, a hobbyist or small scale dahlia breeder can derive great joy and potentially

excellent results with some simple strategies and time spent growing and actively observing their dahlia seedlings, in whatever way makes most sense to them. This book will explore that learning process in a practical way, giving many perspectives, whilst sprinkling in enough science for those interested in optimising and personalising their outcomes with some foundational knowledge.

There are exciting advancements in dahlia gene science currently happening with the Dahlia Genome Project in the United States. It is likely we will learn a lot more in the coming years about how the dahlia's octoploidal genetics work.

For now, hybridisation of dahlias is still primarily done by hobbyists, enthusiasts and small scale breeders, and the way we make sense of the diverse outcomes of our seed-grown dahlias is through making predictions, trial and error, observations, record keeping, and then trying it all over again.

We can be grateful to two centuries of dahlia hybridisers who carefully selected certain traits and bred the recognised types and forms we have today, and it is thrilling that from this foundation we can mix and match those genetics and generate completely new and unique dahlias each time we grow from a dahlia seed.

At left: large seedling vs pompon   Above: diverse range of genetically distinct dahlia seedlings

Cloned Dahlia Plants vs Growing from Seed

Before we go any further it would be useful to establish the difference between growing a "named cultivar" or cloned dahlia and that of growing a dahlia from seed.

When it comes to propagating dahlias, there are two very different ways to create a new plant.

Dahlias can be grown as clones, where the new plant is an exact genetic replica of the parent. This is most commonly done by either dividing up a tuber clump (each section must have a viable growing eye, and access to the food source in the tuber), or taking cuttings from either a tuber shoot or actively growing plant and striking those cuttings to form new roots and create an independent plant. Growing a cloned plant is know as asexual propagation. It gives a predictable result and a bloom that is identical to the parent plant.

Alternatively, sexual reproduction happens when the pollen from one dahlia cultivar (known as the "pollen parent") is introduced to the stigma of a different cultivar (which will become the "seed parent"). This process of pollination initiates the fertilisation of the ovule which then forms a seed. In this instance, half of the genes for the new plant come from the pollen parent, and half from the seed parent, and in the complex blending of their octoploidal genetic structure, the results from seed are very unpredictable. In fact, there are literally billions of possibilities and so each and every time we grow from seed we are creating a new dahlia.

Dahlia breeders, (also known as hybridisers), will do this intentionally, often implementing strategies to increase their chances of generating seedlings that may more closely align with their goals. They then observe the resulting seedlings for several years to assess them against certain criteria, and if they continue to stay consistent and perform well, will potentially release those new cultivars to the world of dahlia growers by using methods of propagation to create more clones.

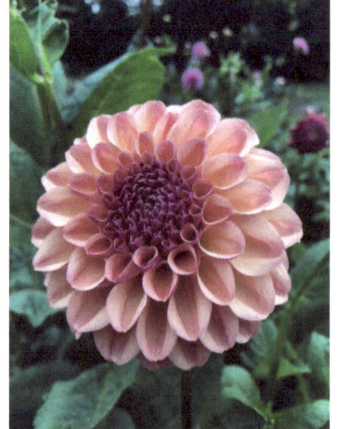

'Breannon' (above) is an Australian cultivar bred by Jenny Parrish. It was the seed parent to 'Serenade Curiosity' as well as all the other seedlings shown on this page. This demonstrates the diversity of resulting colours and forms produced by seed grown dahlia plants.

'Jenny's Treasure' Family Tree

'Jenny's Treasure' Seed Parent

*'Serenade Glimmer'
Grown from open
pollinated seed collected
from 'Jenny's Treasure'*

*Seedlings grown from 3
different open pollinated
seeds collected from
'Serenade Glimmer'*

A Snapshot of the Current Dahlia Growing Culture

Dahlias have undergone a Renaissance in the last decade. Now beloved by so many, the revival has been fuelled in myriad ways. Social media has popularised dahlias, and florists and wedding stylists are using them more often. Also, consumers are seeking out more locally grown produce, building into the "slow flower" movement both for purchasing and growing blooms.

Hobbyists and home gardeners

Being so photogenic, with such diverse range of colours, sizes and forms, dahlias provide endless Instagram content for influencers, growers/farmers and floral designers. The beautiful images become inspiration to new dahlia growers who catch the "dahlia bug" and grow for pleasure in their own gardens. This was exacerbated during covid-19 lockdowns when people found themselves with more time for home-based hobbies, in particular, gardening.

Floral Stylist Demand

Even though they have a relatively brief vase life of 3-7 days (depending on the cultivar), dahlias have become increasingly popular in floral design, especially for weddings and special events. The growth in market demand for dahlias has encouraged growers to establish micro flower farms and grow dahlias as their primary crop.

Furthermore, the relatively long flowering period of dahlias on the farm makes this flower preferable to labour-intensive, short-lived annuals when growing on a small scale. The short vase life of dahlias can even be an advantage to micro farms with the transport logistics and costs making locally grown dahlias preferable to imports.

Only a decade or so ago, dahlias were seen as unfashionable, impractical or unavailable, but now are a staple in the florist trade.

Flower Farmers Direct Retail

Additionally there has been a shift by consumers to preference local, seasonal, sustainably grown blooms for myriad other reasons (reducing flower miles and chemical sprays and in supporting local economies), which has been assisted by the ease in finding farmer-florists directly. This connection between consumer and producer also allows for bespoke customisation, with brides and consumers requesting unusual dahlia colours and bloom forms that weren't available in the past. Small farms have the capacity to be more boutique and experimental in which of the dahlias they grow, not having to plant hundreds or thousands of a single cultivar to maintain commercial viability, but rather trialling smaller numbers of newly bred dahlias that provide a point of difference and signature palette direct to the customer.

Dahlia Society and Exhibitions

The world of Dahlia societies and annual exhibitions and competitions are generating more interest than ever, and the focus on growing to the standard of excellence required to become a grand champion and win a blue ribbon on the head table keeps the established dahlia forms from deteriorating. Generations of breeding work has formed the foundation of most of the dahlias we have been able to access in the last decade or so, and there are many dahlia breeders focused on developing new dahlias that adhere to the show standards. The complex genetics of dahlias and perpetual cloning can lead to genetic deterioration over time. This is compounded by the prevalence of virus which can reduce vigour. For these reasons it is important that breeders continue to introduce fresh cultivars in established show forms as well.

At left and above - selection of mixed seedlings from Serenade Farm

How has this recent popularity affected the industry?

The sudden flourishing and widespread popularity of dahlias has lead to frenzied online buying of tubers over winter and spring with buyers desperate to accumulate all the cultivars on their wishlist and nab the current year's "unicorn" dahlias (the ones most desired and in low supply). The business of supplying dahlia tubers (and more recently cutting-grown plants) has consequentially also exploded, with a huge number of new suppliers, farms, and hobbyist side-hustles coming online to try to fulfil demand.

Many small flower farms rely on tuber sales as part of their annual income, to fill the cashflow gap in the winter season when their cut flowers are not in season. Being able to provide the most desirable cultivars or having exclusive stock of new releases has become the key to the success of this model, especially with the exponential increase in farms offering the more standard readily available dahlia tubers for sale.

It follows then, that if one could hybridise one of the next dahlia "unicorns" they would be at a distinct advantage when selling tubers/plants. As such, there has also been even more value placed on breeding and growing from seed that has been generated from this rise in the popular interest in dahlias.

Many gardeners or micro farmers who have been put off by the so-called online tuber sale "Hunger Games" or frustrated by exponentially rising costs, frequently misidentified tubers, and questionable quality from some suppliers, are looking for alternatives. For these growers, learning to collect their own seed and explore the possibilities that lie therein, is something that appeals as an alternative.

Regardless of your journey into and experience with growing dahlias, or the reason for your motivation to explore the world of growing from seed, I hope that this book can further pique your interest, and cultivate curiosity in what you might find when you roll the genetic dice of this intriguing flower and grow from seed.

Let's learn a bit more about the science of growing dahlias!

At Right and Above - popular seedlings growing on Serenade Farm for florist orders

Where to start?

Germinating a dahlia seed is one aspect of breeding a new dahlia. In a way it is the first step, but it is part of a continuous process which cycles with the seasons.

• Germinate seed in Spring.
• Nurture plants to bloom by late Summer.
• Assess blooms against your personal assessment criteria and decide which to keep or breed from, or to discard
• Observe, keep records, and reflect on future goals and planting plans
• Hybridise and collect more seed for next season in Autumn.
• Dig, divide and replant tubers or cutting-grown clones of your seedlings to develop further, or named cultivars for future hybridising in Winter, while you also plan and dream..
... and the cycle begins again the following Spring

Depending on where you are in your season, and in your dahlia journey, you may jump in at whatever step makes most sense to you at that time.

Understanding the continuous flow of the process means that you can always reflect on where the dahlias have come from and what their potential might be, and appreciate and explore what you have at the time too.

Left 'Serenade Whisper'
Right, Sibling seedlings from the open pollinated seed parent 'Lileah Pink Petticoats'

Growing Your Own Dahlias from Seed

Dahlia Seed Science

I know you're keen to get into germinating and growing your seed, but I'm going to sneak in a little science first, as this understanding can inform so much about growing, and certainly will be helpful in understanding more about hybridising and collecting your own seed and what to expect.

Dahlias are from the plant family Asteraceae (the "daisies") and as such have what is termed composite flower heads. This means each bloom that we see is actually a cluster of tiny little individual florets or inflorescences. There are the disc florets in the middle that are each a reproductively perfect flower and generally form the seeds. Around the outer parts are the ray florets that we commonly call the petals. Those outer inflorescences are most often infertile and biologically function only to attract the pollinators.

As we briefly touched on, unlike most plants that are diploids in their genetic structure (i.e. 2 sets of chromosomes and predictable dominant/recessive genes), dahlias are octoploids. Their staggering 8 sets of chromosomes, half inherited from seed parent and half from pollen parent, give a complex blending of traits including the colour, size, petal shape, form and arrangement.

In addition, since the dahlia bloom is a composite flower, each of those tiny centre disc florets are fertilised by a distinct pollen grain and form a genetically unique seed. Even from the very same seed pod that is hand pollinated with pollen from one other selected cultivar, (so the same seed parent and the same pollen parent) the resulting plants are genetically different from one another.

Without geeking out on mathematic probabilities and complex genetic theory going into alleles and chromosomes, suffice to say that for the nuanced combinations of traits, there are literally billions of possibilities. Each new plant will be distinct and unique, and given that the less common gene expressions can be "hidden" in the parents, with enough rolls of the dice it is possible to discover some very visually novel blooms. This doesn't for a moment mean that every new dahlia is amazing and worth keeping and will be the very next "unicorn", but the possibilities are intoxicating!

Above - dahlia showing disc florets in centre and ray florets (or "petals") surrounding them
At Left - handful of dahlia seeds, some sprouted

Due to the fact that dahlia blooms are composite flowers, the very highly petalled double, giants, ball or pompon dahlias are often a little more challenging to get much seed from since most of their florets are the infertile decorative petals. It is relatively easier late in Autumn (during shorter days) when the petal count is reduced and the centre "blows" or "opens" more quickly, to hybridise with those forms.

Conversely, types such as singles and collerette dahlias, with far fewer petals, readily make much more seed, since there is a big open centre with many disc florets, surrounded by a single row of ray florets and plenty of pollen to attract the bees and other pollinators. They are also far simpler to access when first experimenting with hand pollination.

The time it takes to go from bloom to mature seed is around 4-6 weeks.

Disc florets visible

Pollen and stigmas ripening

Seed forming in pod

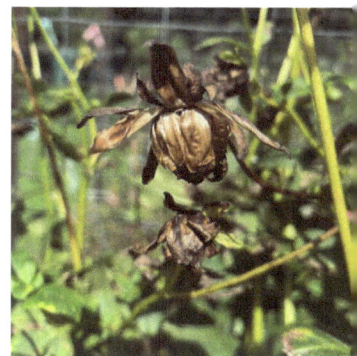
Mature seed pod

Left to form seeds naturally, a dahlia bloom opens completely, exposing the centre disc. These disc florets will first produce pollen from the anthers ("male" part). The pollen ripens gradually over 3-4 days from the outside of the bloom inwards. Then the disc floret stigmas ("female" part) become receptive later.

Mostly self-infertile, dahlias prefer to receive pollen from a genetically different dahlia. Insects act as vectors, moving pollen from flower to flower. Humans can also intentionally control which pollen gets to which flower. We will explore methods for doing this in the chapter on Intentional Hybridisation. Regardless of how it gets there, when ripe pollen lands on the stigma, it travels down the tube of the stigma to the ovary, where it fertilises the ovule, and this is what will form the seed, combining genes from both dahlias to form a unique genetic code.

It then takes several weeks for this fertilised ovule to grow inside the seed pod, and it thickens and darkens during this time. The old petals wither, usually falling to the ground. When the seeds have matured, the whole seed pod turns brown and dries out.

In our very long subtropical climate season here on Serenade Farm (at least five months of blooms), I start hybridising in mid-Autumn, two months prior to the expected end of season. A hard frost will end the season if you are in a colder climate, but for us, it comes with gradual die-back due to short day dormancy triggers.

It is also worth noting that producing seed is an energy sink to the plant, so it can affect tuber quality and size, and also once the plant has set a lot of seed it may slow down bud production. This is another reason it may not be wise to do much seed production early in the season.

Dahlias in late Autumn starting to blow their centres for easier pollination

Harvest and storage of your own seed

All going well, by the end of Autumn you will have mature pods of seed on your plants. If you need to harvest early, first check for viable seeds in the pod by feeling around and gently squeezing, or you can peel back the outside layers to have a look. If seeds are dark and firm they are likely mature and you can open up the pod and spread out thinly paper to dry.

If they are not completely mature but you are forced by extremely wet cold weather or frosts to cut early, give them the best chance by placing stems in a vessel of water indoors (like a vase of flowers). You won't necessarily achieve the same levels of viability from all seed, but if you have no other option, it's worth a try.

Keep track of at least the seed parent if possible, and then separate out the plump, firm, viable seed from the chaff. Small amounts of seed can be separated by hand, or larger amounts can be winnowed either via traditional methods, or by constructing a small-scale seed cleaner (excellent DIY plans are available on the internet). and then when completely dry, you can store the seed in a airtight container in a cool dark place.

It is best if you are able to use your collected seed the following spring, as germination rates are best in that first season using fresh seed.

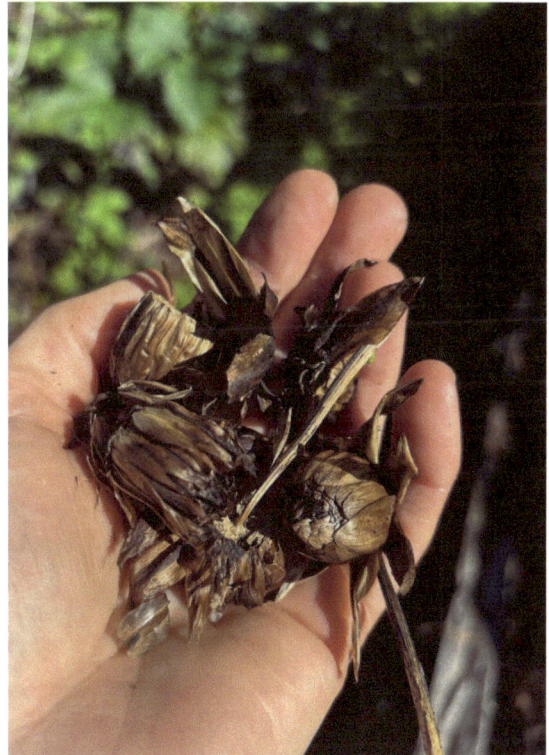

Top right: Almost ripe seed pod with firm dark seeds visible when outer layers peeled away
Above right, handful of dry mature seed pods

Sourcing Dahlia Seed

Whether it be with your own carefully curated, hand collected seed, or with any dahlia seed you manage to source, you can get started with growing your own dahlias.

If it's not the right time of year to collect dried pods from your own Autumn garden, or you haven't grown dahlias before, perhaps connect with a dahlia-growing friend or neighbour, or purchase seed from a specialist dahlia farm or home gardener enthusiast from your local garden club.

Ideally source seed collected from the types of dahlias that you like best, as although we've established you'll get a lot of variation, that is the first step in growing something you will like. There is a lot more to it than that of course, since the unknown pollen parent will also be contributing half the genes to your new seed, but let's keep it simple for now.

If you do buy cheap large scale commercial dahlia seed packs from a nursery, you might find the results a little underwhelming. But if you find yourself in Spring and that's the only seed you can find, you can certainly use that to practise with for now.

Above images: self-collected seeds from Serenade Farm

Trays of dahlia seedlings in early Spring

Germinating Dahlia Seeds

When do I start my seeds?

Dahlias are naturally a summer/autumn flowering plant. We start our seeds in Spring to give them time to establish into a mature plant through spring and early summer and to be flowering at their best as the longest days start to shorten.

So it depends on your specific climate - start your seeds no more than 6 weeks before you predict it will be safe to transplant them out into the garden (or into large 30cm (12") pots if you prefer to grow in containers). If it is still quite cold, or you might get an unexpected frost, you may need a protected place to germinate and grow them. If your starting date is before Spring Equinox you might also like to grow them under extended daylength with artificial grow lights, it just helps them get established well.

Generally as long as you get them out into the garden by Summer Solstice (we'll talk about dahlia's photoperiodism, or day length sensitivity in the next section) you'll have plenty of time to see them bloom, assess several flushes of flowers and for the plants to form a tuber clump by the end of the season.

Top: Seedlings started in Spring planted in 72-cell trays getting some early morning sun

How long will it take my seeds to sprout?

Dahlias are not difficult to germinate, but it's a quirk of some dahlias to have a staggered germination rate, where the first to sprout may happen in just a couple of days, and others from the very same pod can take much longer. I took careful records of germination rate of a batch of 2000+ seeds that were all started on the same day, and I still had a small number of seeds only just breaking through their casing on day 72! In previous years I had given up after about a month.

The reason I was keeping records was to test a hypothesis I had heard that the longer a dahlia seed took to germinate, the more likely it was to produce a fully double bloom. However, my results showed no correlation.

What germination methods are best suited to my climate and conditions?

Ideally use fresh seed, collected the previous Autumn and stored in very dry, cool conditions. To germinate you need to introduce enough moisture to initially swell the seed coat, and then keep the seeds only slightly damp but not soaking wet to prevent them either drying out or staying so wet that they rot.

Ideal germination temperature is between 17-21 degrees Celsius (62-70f) and if possible, once sprouted, minimum of 12hrs day length is preferable for the formation of feeder roots. You may find seeds will germinate outside those parameters, but much cooler or hotter temperatures can cause the seeds to rot before they establish, and significantly short days may just slow down critical growth in the first few weeks.

• Direct Sowing:
If you live in a warm climate or wait until this conditions are happening naturally, you can simply direct sow your seeds into the garden in Spring (watch out for snails/slugs though if they are a problem in your garden there are organic, pet-safe pellets that can be used).

• Self-sown:
In our elevated sub-tropical climate (only light surface frosts) here on Serenade Farm, each year I have a number of seedlings popping up by themselves around my garden from seed I missed harvesting the previous Autumn. Typically those plants are some of the hardiest and most vigorous, and prove themselves to be well adapted to our growing conditions. On occasion they even turn out to be some of my favourite seedlings of the season - even more than others grown from seed that was painstakingly hand pollinated!

• Sow into seedling flats/trays:
In a colder climate, or if you'd like to have a little more control or protect them from critters, you can sow seed thinly into seedling flats or trays, but due to the staggered germination rates, it's a good idea to prick them out into individual pots soon after they germinate with a set of true leaves, otherwise later-to-germinate seeds may get shaded out by the first out of the blocks and get leggy or swamped. "Pricking out" is the term used to carefully remove a very young seedling from a communal seed tray or flat, and give it more space and a pot of its own. Be very careful in this process not to damage tender stem or roots.

This page: seeds germinated directly in open trays

• Pre-sprout/Papertowel method:
My preferred method, personally,
is the "paper towel" method, where
seeds are pre-sprouted on damp
paper towel. Each day l remove any
seed that has sprouted and plant into
72-cell seedling trays where each
seedling will grow in an individual cell
so that its roots do not tangle with
others.

By transferring all seeds that
germinate each day, those seedlings
in the same tray are grouped with
others of a similar size. l do keep
them labelled with their seed parent
information too.

The seed raising mix l mix myself
from equal parts vermiculite, perlite
and coco-peat, but any standard seed
raising mix should work fine as long
as it doesn't hold excessive amounts
of water, become hydrophobic, or
otherwise inhibit plant growth. lf
using a sterile mix without fertilisers,
a weak balanced foliar feed can assist
growth. l use a weak fish emulsion/
seaweed solution at this early stage
as a source of Nitrogen and as a root
growth tonic.

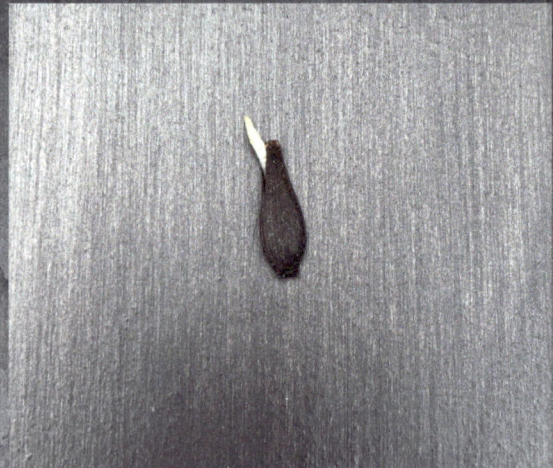

Above - pre-sprouted seed to be transferred into seedling tray at this stage

Below - young seedlings growing under lights

This page - Seeds on damp papertowel
At left - seedlings transplanted into garden

My seeds sprouted, now what?

My seedlings are then grown in my insulated propagation space which has lights set to 14 hrs a day and heat mats that have a thermostat to keep the mix under 21 degrees Celsius. However, this isn't all necessary. I already have this set up for my Spring cuttings and it makes sense to use it for the seedlings as well. A greenhouse, or protected outdoor growing area can be just as suitable as long as conditions within those optimal ranges for the seedling growth.

When they get to around 4 sets of true leaves I will pot up into 100mm (4") pots to grow on, or if the weather is favourable, those small plants can be transplanted into the garden. If you intend to grow your dahlias in pots ensure that you eventually give them plenty of room - typically a 300mm (12") pot would be the minimum size.

Transplanting Your Seedlings
Hardening Off and Plant Depth and Spacing

If you are have chosen to germinate your seeds directly in the garden you can skip this step, but the principles are useful to understand so that you can optimise the growth of your directly sown plants too, as you'll be planting your seeds only 2-3mm deep, but can later mound up around the stem.

If you have raised the seeds indoors or in a protected space, first you will need to get them used to the harsher conditions that they may be exposed to in the garden. "Hardening off" is the process of slowly adapting them to the conditions they will experience outside. You acclimatise them with gradual exposure to natural sunlight and air temperature, as well as winds and rain. You can do this by first exposing them to morning sun, or dappled sunlight, and putting them outside through the day and bringing them back in at night for a few days. Choosing an overcast day to transplant is often helpful, as this can diminish the potential transplant shock.

• Planting depth:
When you transplant your sun-hardened seedlings into the garden, remove a few of the lower sets of leaves and plant them deep in the soil, burying several nodes underground. Nodes are those points along the stem where the leaves emerge, and there are types of cells there that can initiate new shoots or roots. This strategy can facilitate not only additional root development from those nodes, which gives extra stability and access to nutrition, but the possibility that you will get extra tubers forming from those buried nodes.

With dahlias, planting much deeper than the original soil level does not risk the stem rotting, so plant deep down or alternatively mound extra soil (or mulch) high up around the stem during the season.

• Plant Spacing:
Typically dahlias grown from tubers are planted between 300-650mm (12-25") apart. However, due to the unpredictability of growing from seed, you may choose to remove some of your plants through the growing season if they aren't what you are wanting to keep once you see the flowers, so you have the option to plant closer.

When growing from seed maintain that same kind of spacing (as tuber-grown plants) if you are planning to grow all of them for the full season. Alternatively, plant quite a bit closer together if you intend to pull out any plants that don't meet your breeding goals, giving space for the "keepers" to spread out into the gaps between. The advantage of this is that you can grow many more seedlings in much less space. The disadvantage is that it's impossible to predict beforehand which will be the best, and it's not uncommon to get a little cluster of "keepers" growing side by side. Also, shorter-growing plants get shaded out by more vigorous, tall, aggressive plants.

Also there is a risk, if the plants grow very well and are not removed until late in the season, that their roots and tubers can get a little tangled together, and that by removing an unwanted seedling, a good one can have their roots and tubers disturbed when pulling the other out. Planting in pots buried underground can mitigate this, as we'll see with growing pot tubers.

Both pages: Seedlings growing at Serenade Farm

Growing Seedlings as "Pot tubers"

Why would growers leave seedlings in small pots and then bury the plant, with pot and all? It is not uncommon to grow dahlia seedlings this way, and there are a couple of reasons for this strategy.

The first I've already alluded to, being that when removing unwanted plants throughout the season, the bulk of tubers are contained in a pot, and much less likely to get tangled with roots and tubers of adjacent plants.

Similarly, at the end of the season, lifting the mini tuber clump contained within the pot, (known as a "pot tuber") is easy, and it can even be stored, as is, in the small pot through winter. Then the mini clump can be split or replanted as is. Alternatively spring shoots from that pot tuber can be used for cutting material to potentially generate more plants than a traditional tuber clump division.

A third reason for growing pot tubers is that the method tends to produce a compact condensed clump without skinny fragile necks (thin necks can easily snap and become unviable). Not knowing whether the genetic lottery will result in thick or thin necks on our new seedling's tubers, this method can provide mitigation against this possible vulnerability.

Both full page images - various Serenade seedlings

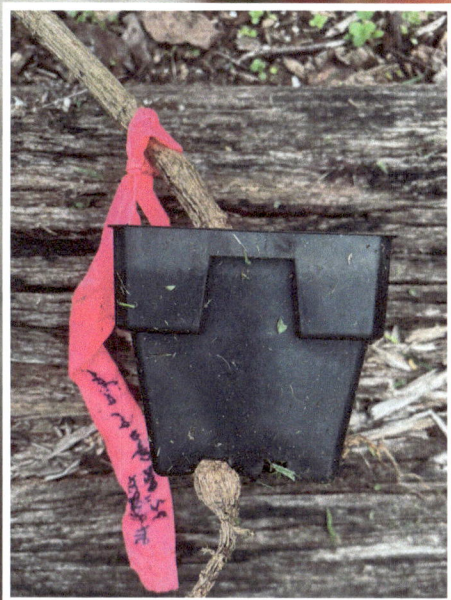

Pot Tuber at end of the season

Dahlia Growing Principles

Growing our dahlias well will not only increase our enjoyment from the experience, but if we are going to assess our seedlings and decide whether to keep them for future years, and possibly share them with others, it is important to give them the opportunity to grow and bloom to their true potential.

There is no single right or wrong way to grow a dahlia, or one-size-fits-all approach. However, there are optimal conditions dahlias require, and the general principles that we will discuss in this chapter can be applied to your specific microclimate and situation. Give them the best balance of sunlight, moisture, temperature, nourishment and physical support that you can, and they are more likely to thrive. Often there will be trial and error involved and regular observation and sometimes troubleshooting. Then we adjust slightly and deepen our knowledge through experience as each season inevitably throws us new challenges.

The previous section took us from seed to a small plant to grow in the garden, but we then need to nurture that seedling well for around 10-12 weeks before we can see the new buds bloom.

The intention of this book is not to be a general dahlia growing guide, as there are many excellent resources that already exist on this topic. Take cues from the chapter on Community later in this book and connect with local growers in your area for specific help for your conditions, or if that isn't possible, I have included details of some other general dahlia growing titles that may assist at the end of this book.

'Serenade Fairylights'

Photoperiodism

Don't fight nature and seasonal preferences - plant in Spring for late Summer/Autumn flowers and dormancy through winter for best success. Even though it is linked, with dahlias this isn't just about temperature and moisture. Dahlias are tied to the seasons via their sensitivity to day length. This is called Photoperiodism.

Certain lengths of daylight, (actually darkness), trigger various stages of growth. As days lengthen in spring, hormone signals are sent to initiate growth and increase feeder root development, especially after Spring Equinox, (days are longer than 12 hours). This puts the plant into an active growth phase. The plant prioritises stem and leaf growth. Whilst the plants may flower before Summer Solstice if the climate is warm enough, most of the energy is used to establish a strong plant. As days shorten again and the nights lengthen, the plants are triggered to start budding up and flower.

After Autumn Equinox when the days shorten below 12 hours, the primary focus is development of tubers and giving the plant ample opportunity to reproduce sexually (producing seeds) with an abundance of flowers. The shorter the days get, the more blooms open their centres for easy access by pollinators. Dahlias will still bloom through the summer months in warmer climates, but typically most cultivars will flower most prolifically in the weeks around and following Autumn Equinox. Consequently, as the days shorten further in late Autumn it is unfair to assess criteria such as petal count, as the blooms are not at their best.

In warm climates, dahlias can be grown through the cooler seasons by augmenting the amount of light in greenhouses with artificial lighting. This seasonal manipulation is only successful with an understanding of their daylength needs.

Supplementary lighting can also be used in late winter/early spring to get an early start on the season by germinating seedlings and growing an established root system ready to plant out when the ground is warm enough. However, understand the impact of changing those things suddenly. For example, be careful if you germinate your seeds indoors under very long "days" (perhaps 14-16hrs under grow lights) and then transplant them out in natural light in short days of Spring. Even though it might be warm enough to grow in the field, the plant will perceive this as a decrease in day length, which can trigger flowering even if the plant is still only very small and without sufficient root system or foliage to support energy production and sustain healthy flowering.

Sun and Temperature

It is not only ambient light levels that affect dahlia growth. Dahlias are a fast growing plant and need a lot of sunlight to photosynthesise and produce energy to flower and set seed. For best flowering they typically prefer at least 6-8hrs of full sun each day. They can still grow in shadier conditions, but will tend to be less vigorous and produce less flowers. Conversely, in some sunny hot climates, shade cloth is used to protect some petal colours from being bleached or damaged by sunburn, or the plants overheating.

However, also consider if you live in a particularly extreme climate, that shade or sun tolerance might be a trait that you choose to select for - we'll discuss that more in our chapter on assessment.

If your garden is shady and you find a seedling that still produces blooms in the shade, then this is a good one to grow more. Or if you discover seedlings that hold their colour and don't discolour in hot sun then they are ideal for your conditions.

The optimal growing temperature for dahlias is 22-24 degrees Celsius. Obviously in natural field grown dahlias there will be substantial variation through the season and they will still grow in a much larger range than this. They won't be in this sweet spot for much of the time, but it's helpful to be aware that when it is significantly colder or hotter than this, dahlias can struggle and at extremes, can go into shock and in particular can wilt dramatically on very hot days. In extremely hot conditions it is best to ensure that although they do have access to moisture in the soil, that they are not overwatered, as the roots won't be able to absorb the water while they are in shock. On the opposite end of the spectrum, very cold temperatures will stagnate growth and dahlias are frost-sensitive, especially the young and developing plants.

Soil and Nutrition

Like most plants, when cultivating dahlias, we try to optimise conditions to have balanced nutrition available on a consistent basis. Although dahlias can be grown in containers (large pots at least 30cm diameter and twice as tall if possible), they will thrive in a healthy, living soil that is high in organic content, microbes and bioavailable nutrients with a balanced to slightly acidic pH. A soil test will ensure that you can amend for any soil deficiencies, but otherwise look for a balanced NPK fertiliser for the early stage of growth and then increase potassium when buds start to form.

It is preferable for stability to plant dahlias very deep, and ideally their feeder roots will extend out in all directions to fill a space of at least 50x50cm and then form a tuber clump around the base of the stem by the end of the season. For this reason compacted soil is not suitable for dahlias. You can build up the soil with well-composted organic material which will encourage worms and other soil organisms to aerate the soil, or some people will initially cultivate heavy soils before planting. However over-cultivation can destroy the natural soil structure, so minimal tilling with the addition of organic matter is often the recommended soil treatment.

Dahlias are heavy feeders, especially when we constantly harvest blooms over a long season. Even with a rich soil you may like to add pelleted fertilisers and/or give regular foliar feeds (fish emulsion, potassium rich foliars, seaweed tonics).

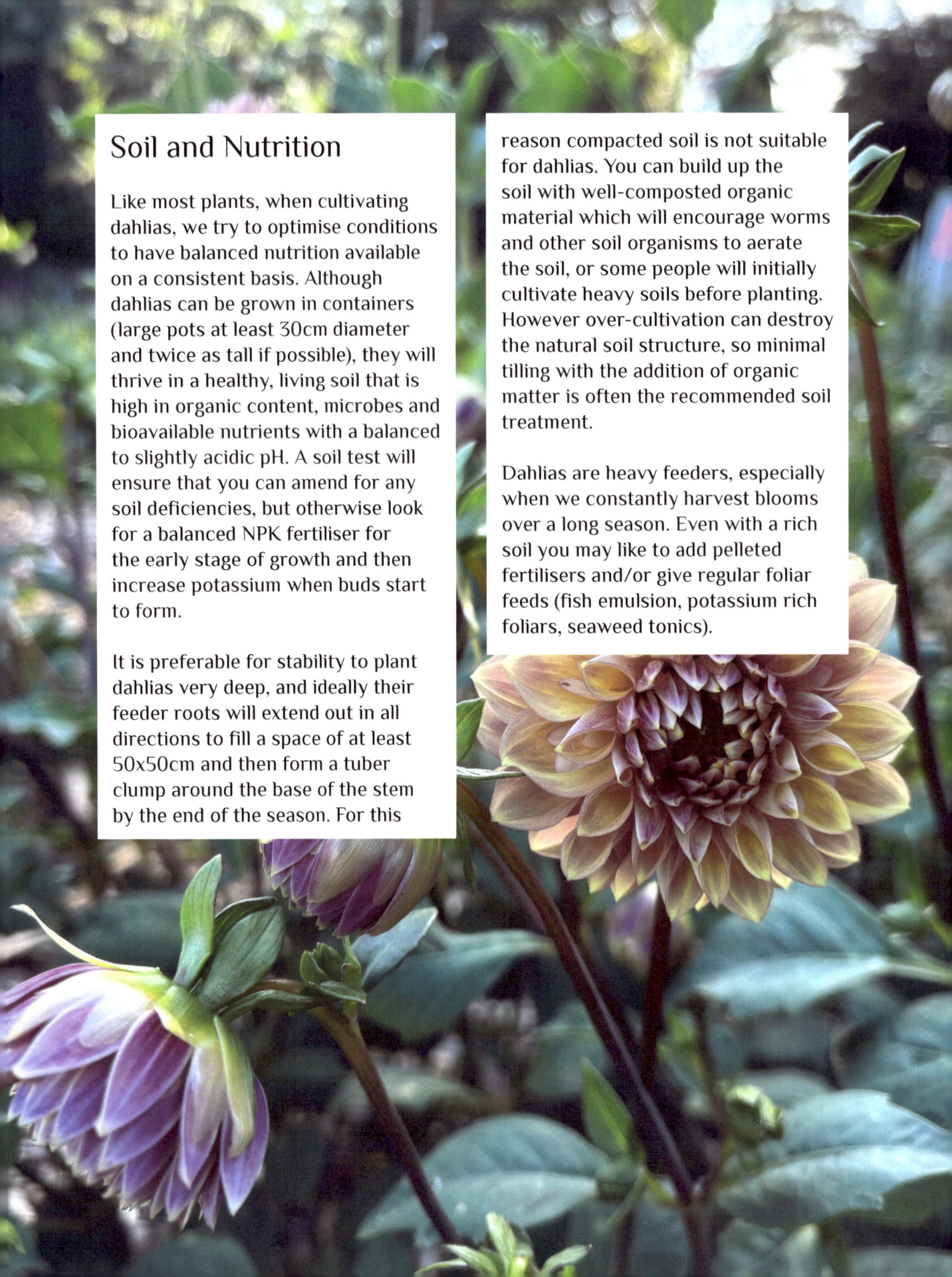

Moisture and Air Balance

One thing dahlias do not take kindly to is wet soggy feet. Seedlings tend to cope marginally better with a heavy soil than tuber-grown dahlias, since they establish a strong root system before tuber-grown plants, and don't risk rotting to the same degree. However, it is still important to have a well-aerated soil, so this is where building up raised beds, and ensuring adequate drainage is imperative to successful dahlia growing, especially if you have a wet summer in your climate.

The amount and timing of your watering will depend very much on your specific climate and soil. In very free-draining soils you may need to water frequently so that the soil doesn't completely dry out too often, in humid areas you should concentrate watering early in the day so that the leaves don't remain too wet and tend toward fungal issues on the foliage.

Pests and Diseases

When we bring exotic plants like dahlias into our gardens we invite all manner of challenges - insects, virus, bacterial and fungal infections and more. In most cases the best preventative is to keep our plants as healthy as possible, by optimising light, sun, nutrition & moisture conditions. When plants are nutrient deficient, or water stressed, they are going to be more susceptible to pest and disease issues.

It is difficult to assess a seedling that is heavily affected by mite damage, or chewed by caterpillars. It is inevitable that during the season one or more of these issues will arise, so learning to manage these challenges becomes essential to effectively growing and breeding dahlias. You will find some seedlings tend to resist infection, or attack by certain pests, and these seedlings are likely to continue to do well in your specific micro-climate, and are worth nurturing.

Also educate yourself on the signs and symptoms of virus, fungal and bacterial infection, some of which cannot be treated, and plants are best removed before spreading throughout your collection. Whilst there was some misinformation being circulated that no virus could be passed on through seed, that is unfortunately incorrect.

My personal strategy is always based on a foundation of soil health and diverse biology to keep everything in balance. We have a thriving eco-system with frogs, reptiles and other natural predators being great assets to our pest control.

Structural Support

Giving tall dahlia plants some form of physical support (stakes, trellis, ties, corralling, horizontal flower netting) is fairly common when growing in a garden, on small scale or for exhibition growing. Your decision to do this or not with your seedlings would be influenced by your goals, method, and also scale. Personally, one of my assessment criteria for cut flower farm seedlings is for self-supporting plants and that only need minimal assistance staying upright. Therefore l want to see that trait in the seedlings that l keep on. l also plant close and remove plants through the season, so l don't give my seedlings much support. l do corral them with rope down either side of the double-planted rows, and being planted close (20cm) also encourages them to grow upward (but not always). The disadvantage with not giving the plants adequate support is that it can be more difficult assess other criteria such as stem strength and position if the plant is not supported. So decide what works for you, but be aware this is something that may need to be considered.

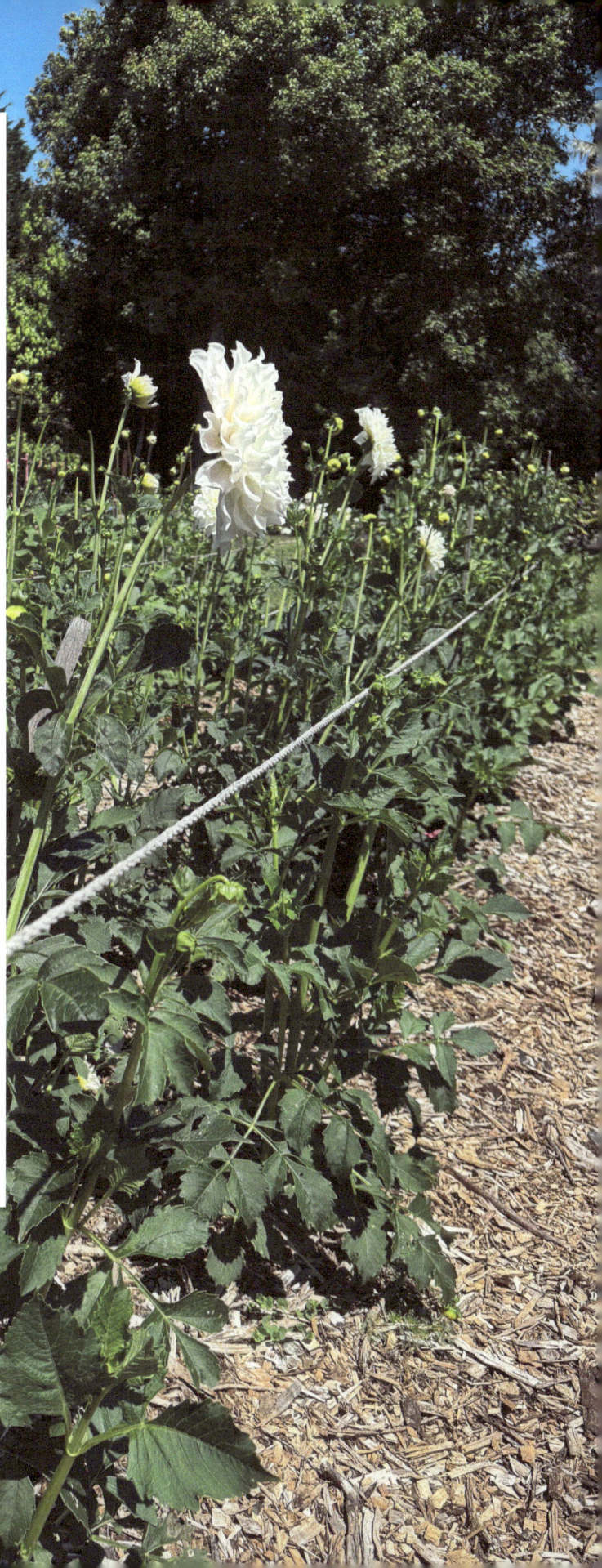

Get Curious About Your New Dahlia Seedlings

So you've germinated your seed, grown and nurtured your plant for 10-12weeks and the first bloom opens. Witnessing this first unique bloom to ever exist is such a delight. Other dahlia breeders describe it as being like Christmas morning to see the newest blooms as they slowly unwrap themselves from their little buds. For me, though, l liken it to meeting a new friend. There is the first impression, and then deeper understanding and appreciation grows as you get to know them more over time. Then after the period of dormancy, when you grow them in subsequent seasons it's like seeing a dear friend after they've been on holidays for the winter!

We are going to dive down the fascinating rabbit hole of seedling assessment in this chapter, but before we do, it's important to establish that there simply is no right or wrong, no objectively good or bad when it comes to a seedling. A brand new dahlia seedling simply is, and we can look at it and ascribe valence to it in reference to our individual context and our goals. Whether it is worth keeping (or it isn't) depends on our personal taste and objectives.

However, there tends to be two different types of assessment criteria. There are the aesthetic considerations which include colour, form, petal shape and arrangement, and to a degree bloom size, that are for the most part subjective. Then there are the traits that we assess that are more functional in nature - the health and structure of the plant, strength and length of stems, head attachment and position. The latter can be nuanced depending on your personal goals.

It can be challenging at first to assess critically, but l encourage you to develop observation skills enough to be discerning, and to be able to give valued assessment of your new seedlings. Stay curious, think about why you are wanting to grow from seed and what you'd like to see in your garden.

Left & Above, various seedlings currently under assessment

Breeding for Exhibition?

The societies have already defined assessment criteria for you. Simply get a copy of your show judging standards and learn how to recognise the forms and petal shapes, and also some sizing rings to measure mature blooms. This can take practice, knowing what to look for and actually seeing the nuance, so it's definitely beneficial to seek out a mentor in your local society if this is your goal.

Growing from seed for your own personal garden with no clear goals?

Use the ideas in this section to learn to observe your new dahlias. Get curious and actively notice the similarities and differences, the traits that make each dahlia unique from another. If nothing else it will help you truly appreciate all the little details, quirks and unique character of each bloom, which can be a delight in itself.

Growing with a goal in mind?

Take time to note down, in detail, the traits that you like most, or that best suit you and your growing style and objectives. Articulating this clearly will assist your decision making process regarding the type of seedling you would like to keep, develop and grow year after year, and potentially share with others. It's more than likely that this may evolve and change over time, so your first iteration doesn't have to be perfect - just start formulating an impression of your "ideal dahlia" so that you can move in that direction.

It gets much easier to assess your seedlings over time. I'm sure this is facilitated by the compounding nature of dahlias and the limited amount of time and space most of us have to grow them! At the end of each season that one tiny seed has magically turned into a whole clump of tubers. If you choose to lift and divide them then you might have twice to ten times the number of plants of that particular seedling, not to mention a handful of seeds as well. I'm sure you can imagine how quickly this can escalate to a garden heaving with dahlia plants, squished into every available nook and cranny. This compounding scale and the amount of work it takes to dig, divide and replant tubers, certainly helped me make some of the tougher decisions as to which plants to keep or let go.

Goal 1: My Perfect "Wedding Bouquet" Dahlia for the farm

* ballet pink with petal shimmer, gold tips, no discolouration in sun
* medium width/length petals, mostly involute
* ball-like in form but with flatter front
* outrageously amazing stems & head attachment
* facing 60degrees or higher
* tight packed, very high petal count
* self-supporting plant
* pumps out blooms all season long
* no green centres in hot summers
* produces heaps of tubers with short strong necks, that store well
* Healthy, robust plant that resists Broadmites and other pests

Far right, self-supporting plants that don't need staking   *Above: write a list of desired traits*

Just as a simple example of one minor trait I breed for and why.
Here on Serenade Farm we grow a large volume of plants for cut flowers (in addition to our breeding program). With just two of us engaged in this we look for ways to streamline tasks, and one way we do this is by not individually staking every plant, but rather by corralling each bed with ropes around the edges of the double rows. Fortunately we are fairly protected from strong winds, so this is workable, but it's still advantageous for our plants to be self-supporting. We do employ cultural practices to keep them compact (planting very deep, mulching high, harvesting stems low down to create low centre of gravity), but some plants are just genetically better equipped to grow long straight stems even in identical conditions. Some plants are naturally "sprawlers" and have a tendency to spread horizontally and need a lot more support. So the requirement for a upright plant habit is far more important to me than it might be to someone who is happy to stake each plant individually.

Get Curious about... Wow-Factor

Sometimes there is just something about a seedling that sets it apart. It can be almost undefinable. You can explore and observe each of the aspects that we will discuss in this section, take notes, and keep records, and learn as much as you can about each new dahlia you have created by growing that tiny seed, but this goes beyond ticking boxes. Each time you look at it in bloom, it takes your breath away or makes your heart sing. It can unlock a moment of awe, or create an escape from everyday life and light you up with it's unique qualities.

On the flipside, I've had blooms that might score well for my criteria in every category I outline in this chapter on assessment, but I find myself a bit ambivalent about it for some reason. Those ones tend to find their way to friend's gardens where they are better appreciated for their subjective beauty in someone else's eyes. But when creating your own method of assessment, or list of criteria, you might like to consider one line in there for wow-factor. I don't keep many that don't score well in everything else on my personal list of breeding criteria, but there are always a couple of odd-balls that just steal my heart.

When defining my breeding goals, there is a joyous category of seedlings that I keep and breed for that are purely for learning, discovery and a self-indulgence - I love to take hold of those threads of curiosity and see where they lead, even though it's not always sensible to do so.

My 'Serenade Curiosity' (photo opposite) was the first to seed this feeling in me, and since then a few others have also piqued my interest to that degree.

Left: 'Serenade Curiosity'   Above - various seedlings under assessment at Serenade Farm

Get Curious about... Colour

Although it seems like it may be a simple trait to observe and assess, colour in dahlias can be complex and nuanced.

Some blooms have clear even colour throughout, and it's simply a matter of working out how to describe that colour. However, observe the blooms through seasonal changes - varying daylight hours, overcast days or bright sunlight, nutrition available to the plant to form pigments. All of these and more can contribute to how the colour is expressed each time your seedling blooms.

In addition to natural variations possible in our own garden, the same cultivar grown in different gardens and climates can vary significantly.

Getting curious with paint sample cards

To get my head around all those different colour variations, my preference is to group into just a few small "bins" initially, so that l can get a feel for which colours are over-represented in my seedlings and/or which l seem to be missing. This also comes back to my objectives to have a well rounded cutting patch full of healthy seedlings that can fulfil all my florist cut flower orders.

As well as taking photos, in my field notes l describe in terms of saturation (either low, mid or high) and then whether it is a cool or warm tone and then basic hues like red, yellow, orange, pink, purple, or white.

However, l have found that this is only the beginning when it comes to observing colour, and that l invariably end up with a lot of seedlings that don't fit neatly into any simple colour category.

Contrasting colour on reverse of petals

Gold petal tips

Front edges of petals with contrasting colour

Picotee - defined outline around each petal

Variation in colour on each petal

Variation in colour between petals

Individual petal with burgundy centre and white outer

As you can see from these examples, dahlia blooms often don't have a single consistent colour. Take time to observe your seedlings for distinctive colour patternings that may get inherited frequently by their seedlings.

Each petal outlined with white

Look for contrasting colours between front/reverse of petals, or a gradation of colour from tip to base. Some dahlias even have a contrasting "outline" around each petal, known as a "picotee". A touch of gold or white on the tip of each petal is another trait that l see often in certain lines of seedlings. When you observe your seedlings also look out for ombré or gradient fades from one related colour to another, or for the more dramatic and obvious bi-colours with more vivid contrast or streaks, stripes or spots, stonewash or watercolour-type effects.

When exploring and assessing the colour of your blooms it helps to look at both the whole bloom, as well as pulling blooms apart to observe individual petals and you can see the way the pigments vary across single petals or between different petals.

Individual petals with contrasting colour

This fascinating dahlia is 'Lileah Pink Petticoats'. It was hybridised by the Australian dahlia breeder, Kate Mungoven. Kate was kind enough to share this new cultivar with me, to assist in my breeding goal of producing fully double dahlias with petaloids.

In addition to producing many seedlings with petaloids, a distinctive colour patterning has been passed on to such a large number of new seedlings both as a seed parent and through pollen, that has become almost more of her genetic signature than the petaloids themselves.

In particular, I was intrigued in the way that even though overall the pigment saturation and intensity varied, they all displayed the same mix of pink with orange striping and patches, whether it be with bright, highly saturated pigments, down to a very subtle pastel version or even in one case the same patterning with only white and yellow pigments present.

'Lileah Pink Petticoats' was seed parent to seedlings above, and pollen parent to those below. Despite varied form, there is a commonality of colour patterning.

There is a large decorative cultivar in Australia named 'Winkie Cinnamon'. (pictured) It is well known for its muted spicy orange tone. When I first grew it in my subtropical climate the colour was a highly saturated hot pink. I presumed I had been sent a mislabelled tuber, since I couldn't reconcile the bloom I was growing with any photo I had seen of it grown in cooler climates. However, as the season progressed and we moved into the cooler autumn months, the more typical tones started to reveal themselves, and it was clear that something about our conditions had caused the colouring. Colour in your dahlias isn't always fixed, so ensure you observe and record colour, like the other traits, throughout the season and over the years of assessment.

Early season 'Winkie Cinnamon'

The well known wedding favourite cultivar 'Cafe au Lait" ranges between a neutral coffee-cream to a soft baby pink, with streaks of purply pink on the reverse of some petals. This is all on the same plant growing in the same soil, and sometimes at the same time of year. The determining factor for this seems to be the amount of light that the bud is exposed to as it develops, and the sensitivity must be quite high, affected perhaps by an overcast day, since the same plant can have flowers at slightly different opening stages expressing the different colours.

I have observed the same variations arising from some seedlings of 'Cafe au Lait' where the cream/pink colour variation has been inherited. I have a cultivar in my own breeding patch, 'Serenade Symphony' (pictured here) that carries this same colour variability trait.

Hang on - my flower suddenly changed colour!

Beyond the slight colour variations outlined on the previous page, sometimes a dahlia suddenly appears with a bloom that is a dramatically different colour to a previous one that you've observed. There can be a couple of explanations for this.

Before you get too excited and jump to any conclusions, first carefully follow back the stem to ensure that both blooms formed on the same plant. Occasionally 2 stems can arise side by side because either 2 different seeds have germinated, or if you've grown other dahlias in the same area before it might be a sneaky left-behind tuber that was hiding in that spot. However, if you are certain that it is the same plant, it may be a chimera of some type.

A **chimera** occurs when two or more genetically distinct types of cells are growing together in same plant. This is particularly obvious when the chimera relates to colour and we see different streaks, sections or patterns appear on petals due to uneven pigment expression in petal tissues.

A chimera can be stable or unstable. Some stable chimeras are commonly known as "sports" and can sometimes be captured by propagating clones from the specific branch or section of the plant presenting with the new colour.

It is not uncommon for a bloom that presents with a base colour of white, pink, lemon or peach that has burgundy streaks or "speckles" to occasionally give a bloom of all burgundy (or sometimes of all the base colour). Or sometimes the chimera will show as a bi-colour that has uneven patches or segments of a different colour on some blooms but are all one or the other colour on others.

These chimera colour variations can just be a something that will randomly recur and can be caused by a short sections of genetic code that shift around called transposons.

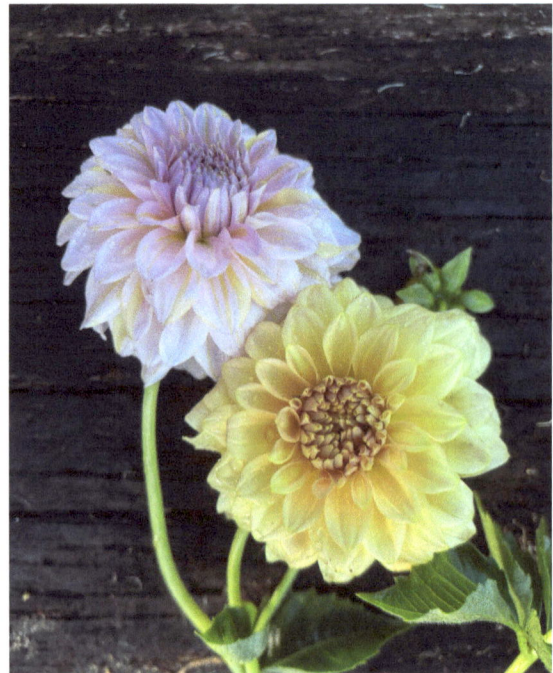

Seedling from same plant showing chimera
At right: different chimera patternings

Reasons for Chimeras include:

• Spontaneous genetic mutation during cell division, known as a "sport"
• Transposons (also known as jumping genes) which are mobile genetic elements in the code that disrupt pigment formation.
• Environmental reasons including temperature fluctuations, virus and other stress-triggered changes
• Virus induced colour breaks especially streaks or mosaic patterns (including Dahlia Mosaic Virus)

Natural plant pigments create colours that we see in dahlia petals. A quick overview of the main polyphenol pigments present in dahlias, and the interplay between them, can help us understand how crossing certain colours might give rise to particular tones.

Polyphenols in dahlias include flavones such as apigenin (pale yellow or ivory contributing to background petal colour) and quercetin (a yellow pigment). Anthocyanin pigments (also in berries) are responsible for red and purple hues and include pelargonin (red to orange) and cyanin (deeper reds and purples). Pinks and other softer tones are created when those otherwise vivid pink/red/purple colours of the anthocyanins are softened with the ivory/yellow hues of the flavones. If the genetic code does not instruct the dahlia to produce any anthocyanins at all, only white and yellow/ivory tones are possible. Sulfurin is also a yellow pigment (recently being studied for its health benefits too). High levels of sulfurin give intense yellows, or if combined with anthocyanin, bronze, peach and apricot tones.

The complex colour variations arise from gene coding for the different biological pigments. Those instructions still need to be triggered in the plant and can be affected by specific nutrients, temperatures, sunlight, and general plant health to synthesise the polyphenols. This is why the same plant, grown in different conditions can vary.

Dahlias do not have the pathways to create delphin to give a blue hue, and so a true blue dahlia is not currently possible. The dark purples that we see in dahlias contain very high concentrations of anthocyanin with very little of the flavones.

It is not just the bloom that can carry pigments either. The stem and foliage and even tubers and seeds can have varying degrees of darker or red/purple pigments to them (caused again by anthocyanins).

Here is another example of colour patterning being carried through the genes:

'Jenny's Treasure' is an Australian cultivar (bred by Jenny Parrish) which has distinctive gold tips on her otherwise bright pink petals.

Below are six seedlings that have resulted from open pollinated seed collected from the 'Jenny's Treasure' breeding line. They have varied colour overall, but each have inherited the gold tip patterning of their seed parent

'Jenny's Treasure'

Above - seedlings that have inherited the gold petal tips from seed parent 'Jenny's Treasure'
At left - highly saturated dahlia seedlings with vivid plant pigments producing those intense colours

Get Curious about... Size

In dahlia society exhibitions, size is standardised and assessed with show rings, measuring overall size of the mature bloom, to judge if they are the correct size for their class. The classifications have terms that whilst they sound general and relative (miniature, small, medium, large), refer to a precise measurements.

It can be quite astounding to see some exhibition cultivars grown up to twice the size you see them in a home garden. Show growers who are aiming to have one perfect bloom from their plant on a specific exhibition date, are diligent with techniques to manage the bloom size (disbudding, disbranching, and careful timing). They are pushing the cultivar to its limits, and carefully controlling conditions to grow them to fit in the size ring for their class.

Clearly, if your objective is exhibition breeding, then size is an important aspect to consider, and you would, again, look up the standards for your relevant society and be growing, assessing and measuring the sizes accordingly.

As I'm not breeding for exhibition stock myself, precise size in those terms is not so important. However, it is still a consideration, as I like to cater to the varied styling needs of my florists.

Whilst I do make notes of the size of my blooms, I record approximate size when growing whole rows of the cultivar for cut flowers, and I'm aware that this often changes through the season.

Also, when I started making notes on my new seedlings, I recognised that there was a dramatic difference between a

10cm (4") tightly packed bloom (which may have been classified as a ball or formal decorative) compared to something open and airy where the back petals flared out or the overall bloom might be very "flat", even though it was the same width. So not only note the width of your bloom, but also consider how deep the bloom is, and the relationship between the two. A pleasing ratio of width to depth might be more significant to your breeding needs than overall size.

When observing size, also consider the relative size of individual petals compared to the overall bloom. There are crossovers here with both form and petal count, which we are yet to explore, but it can influence the perception of size. You might have a 10cm bloom that is densely packed with very narrow short petals, or another that is also 10cm total, with fewer but much larger petals, which will give a completely different look to your tight little compact bloom.

Above: Seedling (left) next to miniature burgundy seed parent and 'Hamari Gold' pollen parent (above right)

Get Curious about... Bloom Form

Dahlia growers new to assessing seedlings often ask for help defining what form their new seedling is. They presume it must be either THIS or THAT, as if dahlias came from the distinct show types and all seedlings can be easily given a classification. The wild species dahlias that our modern day cultivars originated from were tiny simple open-centred, eight-petalled blooms. Everything that has been bred since has evolved from this and the show forms have been refined.

Sometimes seedlings may indeed fall neatly into one of the recognised exhibition forms by adhering to standards for that type. It might be a ball with its uniform involute petals that wrap right around to the stem, or a formal decorative, a waterlily, an exhibition cactus. More often than not, your new dahlia will be somewhere in between.

The "in-between-ness" of otherwise beautiful seedlings make them an easy cull for the exhibition breeder, as would standard "faults" like the presence of petaloids between petals in a fully double bloom. However, if not growing for the society competitions, there's no need to be limited to clear cut forms, colours or other traits that fit in a neat classification box. In fact, some of that same ambiguity is what makes them so appealing. However, it is still useful to be able to describe and understand what you are observing.

All blooms on both pages are seedlings with diverse forms, none of which would fit show classifications

When you look at a new seedling and it falls outside defined forms, how are you going to describe it?

Get curious about the complete shape of your mature bloom as well as the way the petals are arranged and spaced.

Overall, is it round like a sphere, or flat like a plate? Does the centre dome over in a convex way, or perhaps the opposite, does it cup up in a concurve shape like a bowl, with the petals facing upwards?
You may observe that the petals may do a bit of each, with the back petals curving around to the stem, the mid petals straight out to the sides, and the newest petals flicking upwards above the centre point.
Sometimes you might notice that the centre of the bloom protrudes well forward of the rest of the bloom and the back petals flatten back as they open, or that not all the petals are a uniform shape or size.

I found that as I was writing my field notes, I observed in-between or non-exhibition shapes and arrangements that kept recurring, so I invented names for forms that made sense to me. I noted shapes like a "fountain" when the bloom tended to sit more or less horizontally on the top of the stem and petals cascaded down all sides toward the ground - usually when there was a twist or ripple to the petal. I would describe as "dancer" a bloom had petals from the mid range flicking upwards (like the skirts of a dancer as she pirouettes). I've mentioned a "protruding nose" in my field notes, although it's not a trait I like, so often those ones don't even make it to my catalogue of keepers. Other made up descriptors include windswept, pinwheel, or petal swirl, or flicked or rippled petals... all just give me an instant visual in my mind, to classify my seedlings into loose groups that help me get my head around the many new seedlings coming through.

When you grow a lot from seed, you'll often encounter weird odd-balls, and it's up to you to decide if the aesthetic is pleasing enough to explore further.

I won't outline formal exhibition classification terms in this book (ball, decorative, cactus etc), as I encourage non-exhibition growers to avoid using terms that have such clear and precise definitions when growing from seed, unless you plan to conform to those standards. If you are breeding specifically for exhibition, you would need to learn and understand what defines each form that you are breeding toward so that you can assess your own seedlings accurately against those criteria. If not, then I encourage you to learn how to accurately describe your seedlings in meaningful ways that don't necessarily lean on those existing terms.

At right: More unclassifiable seedlings

Another aesthetic form consideration is the symmetry of the bloom. How uniform and balanced is the bloom is across the flower. Certainly any dahlia can have a few mis-fires, but some are genetically predisposed to being wonky and out of proportion in the centre much of the time. I've had some otherwise beautiful looking blooms that are a lovely colour, and pretty petal shape, with great stems, attachment, position, but the uneven centres just make them unpleasing for cut flower production. This bloom to the right was one such seedling, where the majority of blooms on the plant had these uneven centres.

Asymmetric bloom form

Longer layer of back petals in 2 different seedlings

Other form anomalies might be more interesting. I've had several seedlings with a distinctively long layer of back petals. This genetic irregularity likely was the basis of the anemone form as it evolved with selection by breeders over the last 50 or so years, eventually favouring a clear single layer of bigger back petals with small tubular inner petals in the centre.

Anemone form dahlias

At right - 'Lileah Pink Petticoats (centre) who is seed or pollen parent to all surrounding seedlings

Get Curious about... Petal Count, Shape and Arrangement

There is tremendous genetic variation in the petals themselves, not only the arrangement, but the curve, taper, and proportions of the individual petals. It's time to get curious and pull your blooms apart again, this time to take a good look at different petals of both the same bloom, and other blooms to observe details of the petals:

• Curvature: Is the petal flat? Or does it have an inward (involute) or outward (revolute) curve. And do all the petals have an even amount of curve across the entire bloom, and/or does it change from the centre outwards? Some petals can even twist within the contour of each petal giving a rippled effect. Have a look at a few of the examples to see how varied they can be.

• Length vs width of petal: Observe length of the petal both relative to other petals in the same bloom and to other dahlias. Similarly, how wide or narrow is the petal and how does this relate to the length?

• How quickly they taper off at the tip can also vary. Sometimes a petal will gradually go from being wide at the base to easing off to a narrow angle at the top, whereas others will stay the same width all the way along until the tip suddenly tapers off

Similar petals from petaloid seedling siblings

An anemone dahlia with the contrasting petal shapes

Above, below and at right - dissecting blooms to view individual petal shapes , curvature and colours

• Unique petal formations may appear in your seedlings - tubular (fused or curled), quilled, twisted, ruffled petals all can make an appearance, as can little petal-like structures called petaloids that appear within a main petal - either the same colour or a contrasting colour from the rest of the bloom.

• Delicate or robust? Some petals are more delicate and bruise or tear more easily than others, whereas others can tolerate a little rough handling (not recommended, but sometimes it's unavoidable when transporting) For a garden dahlia this might not be a concern, but for cut flower production this is something l need to assess in my seedlings, as bruised petals might make a bloom unusable to a florist.

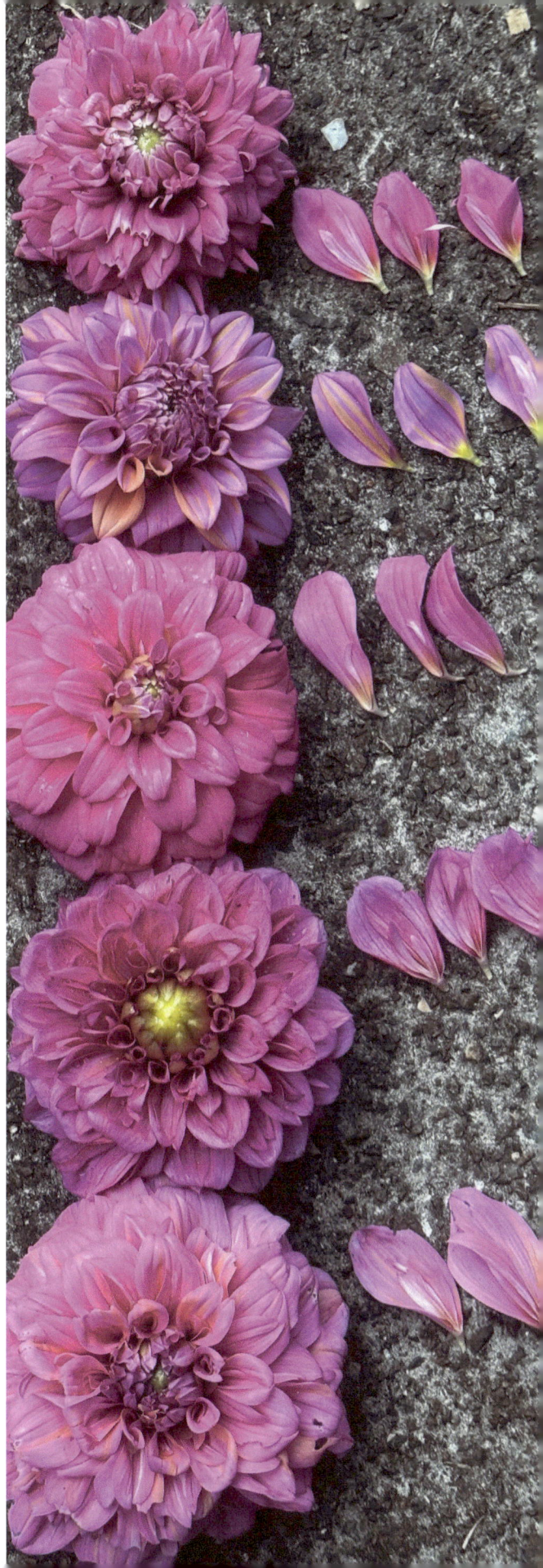

• Petal count and disc visibility:
Petal count doesn't refer to an exact numerical value, but moreso a visual threshold where the bloom has enough petals to hold a tight centre. It is a variable trait even during the season for each cultivar. Short days when the bud is developing will tend to result in a lower petal count, whereas longer days as the bud develops tends to give the bloom more layers of petals, and consequently, a fuller shape.

Besides aesthetic considerations, the significance of petal count is that the lower the petal count, the sooner the central disc will be visible, which is when pollen will start to show. Once pollen forms, the petals start to drop, and so vase life decreases. A trait that many cut flower growers aim for is a high petal count that will hold a tight centre right through the season.

On the flipside, in a hot climate it is possible to have cultivars that have too high a petal count in the heat of summer, which gives the visual effect of a hard green (or golden) centre to the bloom. The heat disrupts the hormone signalling to differentiate the florets into normal "petals" (ray florets) leaving behind hardened green structures or malformed petals in the congested disc. This would be environmentally induced and not necessarily a genetic fault. It is likely this would resolve if grown in a cooler climate. However, if one of your goals is suitability for your climate and you get hot summers, then susceptibility to hard centres might be best selected against.

Some growers prefer the singles, collerettes and other very low petal count aesthetic for their gardens. One advantage is a lot more pollen for insects to access.

Seedling with low petal count and visible centre disc

Seedling with hard centre, common in hot climates

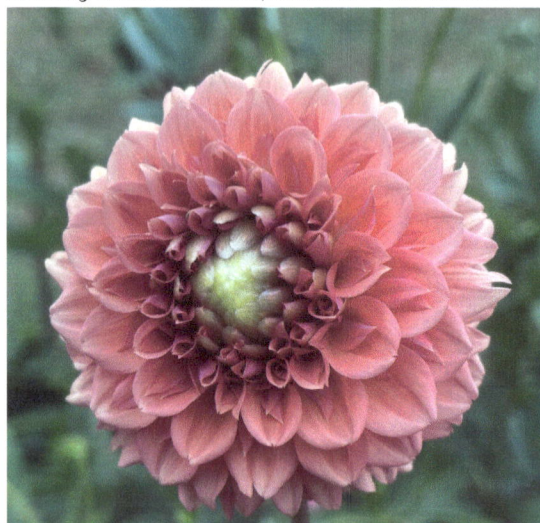

At right: seedling with wide, medium length petals, that are flat to upward cupping and contain petaloids of same colour. Bloom has high petal count, holding a closed centre right through Autumn

Get Curious about... Stem Length and Strength

We're now moving into some of the more functional aspects of seedling assessment.

When breeding for cut flowers, and also to an extent for exhibition, the strength of the stem and its ability to hold the bloom upright is essential.

Dahlia stems can be either solid and rigid, or more fleshy, hollow, or flexible. This trait is more difficult to assess if you are not giving your plants everything they need to grow to their best. For example, plants that are lacking in potassium, or that are suffering from water stress (either too much or too little) may have weaker stems than they might otherwise possess if grown optimally.

We will discuss the overall plant habit (or shape) and height later, but when assessing the stem it is useful to also observe if there are long or short sections between the nodes on your stems. If there are leaves coming out every couple of inches this will give a much bushier plant, but also makes for a lot more work and unevenness in the stems after stripping the foliage if you are growing for cut flowers.

Also, sometimes the main stem of a larger dahlia plant can be too thick to be useful to put in a vase. For cut flowers, I would be ideally looking for nothing much thicker than a pencil but at the same time with enough strength to stay perfectly upright and have no bend at all.

Conversely if you would like a plant that looks attractive in the garden and densely covered in blooms, without any intention of cutting stems for the vase, then having the shorter internodes might be an advantage to your breeding lines, and wide thick stems can be an asset to stability if their cutting potential is irrelevant to your needs.

I do have certain criteria that my cut flower cultivars must pass on, and having exceptional stem strength is non-negotiable. Each time a plant blooms I simply give it a bit of a wiggle and observe how well it holds the head upright. I also observe the stem after cutting, as sometimes they can weaken after cutting, even when treated well.

My grading system is quite simple - in my field notes throughout the season they get classed as "excellent, great, good or fail" but unless there is some very unique trait I am keeping them for it's unlikely that they will pass assessment overall unless they get an excellent on this criteria for the majority of blooms in their first year. Even when they have scored well in the first year they will sometimes fail on this in second year assessment, as I get tougher on this as I go along too.

Anyone who has grown 'Glenmarc Divine', an Australian cultivar bred by Alf Hardingham, would love it for its exceptionally long strong straight stems. (Pictured to the left)

When I grew out 30 open pollinated seedlings from 'Glenmarc Divine', I was astounded not only by the relative consistency of the bloom size and colouring compared to most other dahlias, but that every seedling I grew inherited those incredible long stems (nine of the seedlings shown below)

"Clock-faced" forward head position early season

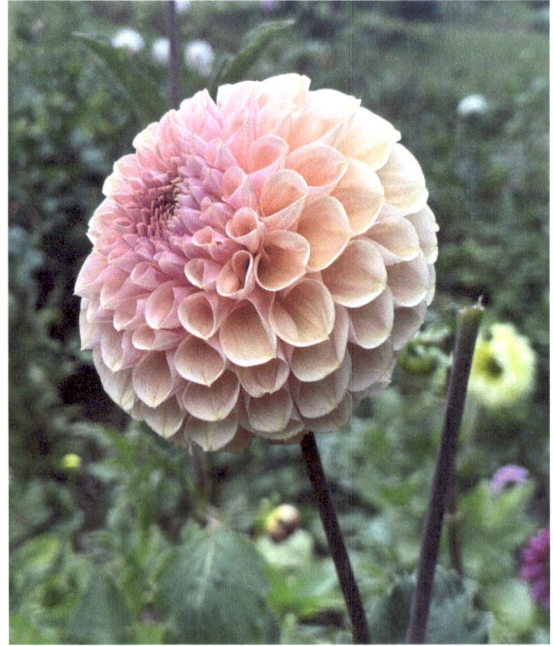
45 degree head position of same bloom mid season

Downward facing head position

'Serenade Curiosity' has poor attachment

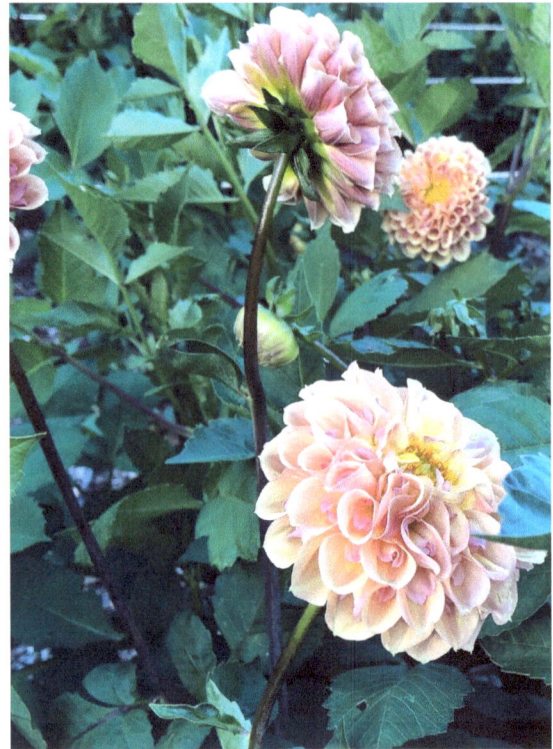

Get Curious about.. Blossom Attachment and Bloom Head Position

We can observe and assess how securely the blossom is attached to the stem. In the extreme, like my little "Serenade Curiosity" seedling, you barely look in its direction and the head will fall off. That is the worst I have ever had, and the only one I have kept, but I have had many others bobble their way to the compost.

The attachment and position are the criteria that in early years I would turn a blind eye to for a pretty flower, just hoping in vain that it might improve in second or subsequent years. Sadly, I've found that it rarely does. However, I do give it a chance during the first season. If the primary bloom is forward facing (with a secure attachment) and then it lifts the head on later stems through that same season, and in that case I will still keep it. The wobbly attachment rarely improves however, so whilst I might give it one or two chances, if it's consistently loose, which often also couples with forward or down facing, then sadly it is rarely chosen to be kept.

Take time to observe the angle and position that the bloom sits on the stem. For cut flowers the degree of tolerance can vary depending how it will be arranged. Generally in market-style bouquets it is helpful for the bloom to angle up and out from the arrangement - so anything from around 45 degrees even to directly horizontal can work.

If being used for large scale arbours or installation, design can often tolerate blooms that are much more forward facing, and even potentially utilise a downward-facing bloom (such as in ceiling mounted hanging arrangements). On the whole, these positions where the bloom is so forward facing it would be called "clock-faced" (like a clock fixed to a wall facing directly forward) or if it nods down to the ground, it has limitations in general floristry, and so personally I wouldn't be wanting to grow on my farm on any large scale.

However, this all still speaks to the individuality of breeding goals and the reasons you are wanting to grow and breed dahlias to begin with. I have a friend who also has a flower and foliage farm and her initial interest in growing dahlias came from being a painter and artist. To her, the most beautiful and paintable blooms are the soft romantic ones that tend to ooze and flow and quite often might droop their head down to reveal all the moodiness of the backs of their petals. She can style these in a vase and paint them and they create the most beautiful floral-scapes.

'Coorabell Jessie' is one of my favourite Australian cultivars, bred by the Wedd Family. (Three images at right)

I have grown out hundreds of open pollinated seed from this cultivar, and seven of the best are pictured alongside the seed parent both front and side view.

In almost every way they were exceptional dahlias, well suited to cut flowers, and these particular seven passed on head position to varying degrees. However, sadly I had to stop using this seed parent, because the vast majority of seedlings would present with a clock-faced, forward head position and therefore had limited functionality for my cut flower orders.

Get Curious about.. Plant Habit

The habit of a plant is its overall shape and structure, including the height, width and branching pattern. Whilst most dahlias will have a similar structure, there will be genetically determined variations that make some more or less suited to your needs.

Typically, a dahlia grown from seed begins with a single stem. Intermittently at what is called a node, two leaves come out from this stem on opposite sides. As it continues to grow, the next pair of leaves emerge at the next node (offset by 90degrees to the one below). Without any intervention, this leading apical tip will keep growing upwards and putting out pairs of leaves until it is triggered to form a bud and flower.

Below - Single stem of unpinched dahlia plant

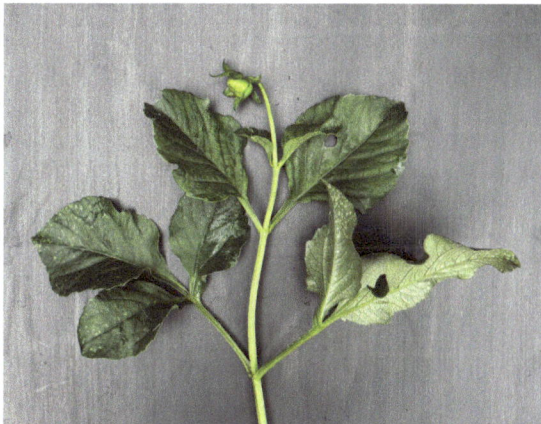

It is common for dahlia growers to "pinch" off that growing tip to "stop" apical dominance, and which triggers (via hormones) the dormant growth bud inside between leaf and stem to grow a new lateral stem. This new branching stem can then form its own bud and flower. By "pinching" or "stopping" the plant, the plant becomes bushier, giving more harvestable flowers sooner and a lower centre of gravity for better stability.

Below - Pinching the apical growing tip

Leaf axial (junction of leaf and stem) where the new axial bud will form a lateral stem or branch

When you are assessing your seedlings, either leave the plant to grow naturally with a single stem to bloom quickly so that you can assess the natural plant habit, or pinch the plant.

Aspects of plant habit to consider:

• Overall height

Dahlias can range from dwarf cultivars of 30cm (12") to tall plants that easily get 2m (6') or more. I've found that when growing from parents that are both tall, it's most common for that trait to be inherited, but occasionally a dwarfed seedling will appear.

• Internodal distance:

As we discussed when looking at the stems of plants, sometimes the distance between each set of leaves can be vast - the longest I measured was 60cm (24") between nodes. Other shorter plants have nodes tight against each other with hardly a gap at all, and very bushy growth with heaps of foliage.

Seedling that reached maximum of 80cm (32") even though both parents were tall cultivars

60cm (24") stem with no nodes (no foliage trimmed)

Bloom on short primary stem being swamped by taller secondary buds

• Short Primary stem

There are some dahlias that will have a short primary bud (at the top of the main stem where the first flower forms) and by the time that bud starts opening, the 2 much longer secondary shoots to each side have shot up and can get in the way of the petals opening. It can be a frustrating trait for cut flower production. This habit is often genetic but can also be the result of growing conditions, so assess through the seasons. You can also pinch out that growing tip to see if that solves the problem. It's an undesirable trait for me, so I'll give it a chance if that's the only issue, but often it will fail assessment based on this trait.

• Oddities

Fasciation is a distortion giving fused stems, extra fused buds or foliage or other deformities to what would be typical growth habit. Often if the fasciation is severe and persists, the plant won't ever flower. However, sometimes it can be caused by stress and is only partial and transitory, and will give normal growth and flowering in time.

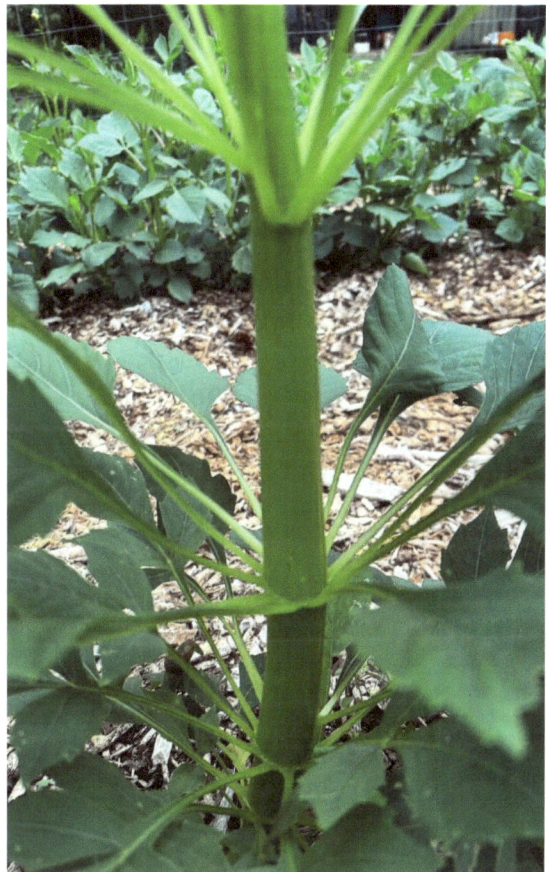

Seedling with persisting fasciation of stem and leaves.

Get Curious about... Floriferousness and Bloom Timing

The tendency to bloom more early in the season, or later, or to have a single big flush, followed by a rest and then another big flush, or in contrast just a nice steady flow of blooms, can be something which is genetically determined. This might not be significant to your growing style or goals, but if your season is short because you grow in a cooler climate with frequent frosts, you may not get enough out of a plant that is slow to take off, and one of the last to start flowering.

If you are timing your blooms for competition or event, you might be looking for a seedling that will be predictable with it's flowering more than the ability for it to pump out the blooms.

If growing for cut flowers, a constant flow of consistent blooms may be a most desirable situation, whereas for garden display, a plant that will be covered in blooms all at once, which can then be deadheaded at their end and then come through with another flush later, may be what you would prefer.

Also, some dahlias will give you many cuttable stems throughout the season, compared to others which are stingy with their blooms. Sometimes there can be a correlation between the bloom size and the number of buds you will get over the season. Some of the giant sizes will tend to only give a few blooms, taking their time to deliver very impressive

specimens. However, this isn't always the case, and some reasonable sized blooms will be very floriferous workhorses all season.

Some dahlia farmers and breeders will keep an accurate tally of how many blooms they get from specific plants to assess this trait, which averaged over a number of seasons is the best way to objectively assess this if you have the time to do so.

As our morning harvests are already quite tight for time in peak season, my assessment of this trait is more intuitive. I'll tend to note first bloom date when I'm first assessing the seedlings so I know if it's an early or late cultivar. I also add comments to my field notes if I notice plants to be particularly floriferous or not throughout the season, especially when growing multiple plants in the second and third seasons.

At right: floriferous seedlings   *Above: cut flower harvest*

Get Curious about... Plant Health, Vigour and Climate Suitability

It is natural to first observe aesthetic traits of the bloom, and even functional aspects such as stem and head position. However, a genetically healthy, strong plant is always going to be preferable to a weak and sickly one, regardless of how pretty the bloom is. This is an important aspect to observe. Some "divas" are worth a bit of extra effort and remedial feeding, but assess your seedling plants and how they compare to one another and other tuber-grown plants, and look for any obvious issues. Genetic health needs to be assessed when the plants are being grown in optimal conditions.

Problems become more obvious in the second year when potentially more plants of each seedling are being grown out. It is likely to be a genetic issue when plants either side of your block of your seedlings are performing better or worse in some way.

Below, healthy robust first year seedling

• Foliage health:
Are leaves consistently healthy and green? There can be a variety of foliage colours and shapes, but sickly yellow colouring or patches or inconsistent colouring throughout the plant when other cultivars either side are doing much better in the same soil might be a indication of a genetic health issue. I had problems with a seedling I observed over 4 years in all different parts of my garden, pots, (and even sent to other growers) that always had very pale new growth. It would green up in time, and the rest of the plant appeared quite healthy, but it was definitely a genetic nutrition issue with that particular seedling.

Below: 'Serenade Whisper' with her genetically determined yellow new growth

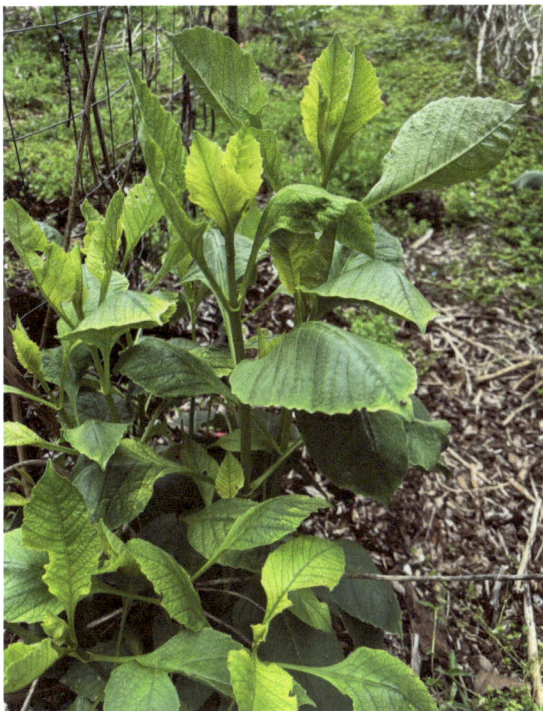

• Pest and disease susceptibility:
It's quite noticeable when growing a block of each cultivar or seedling next to each other that some are always the first and most severely affected by pests like Broadmites. Similarly, some dahlias seem to always be the first to show signs of fungal problems. Whether this is because of foliage characteristics, or how large or dense the leaf cover is overall, or more textured surface for the spores to adhere, or it may be just a general susceptibility. Virus resistance can also be a very contentious issue, as there is quite a range of opinions about this, but it is a trait that some breeders will specifically select for.

• Local climate suitability:
Another advantage to growing your own cultivars from seed is that you are naturally going to be selecting the plants and blooms that perform best in your very specific microclimate. A natural resistance to frost in cool climates, or a heat tolerance, an ability to thrive in humid conditions, or in long stretches of dry without struggling, will naturally happen if you choose plants that are healthier growing in your own garden or farm where those weather conditions are common.

Get Curious about... Ease of Propagation

• Tuber formation/storage:
Some dahlia cultivars are known to be very poor tuber makers and storers. If tuber division is the way you plan to propagate and keep your cultivars over the years, then you need your best seedlings to make good tubers that are ideally a shape that won't be damaged easily, and that have less of a tendency to rot in typical growing and storage conditions.

• Ease of taking cuttings:
Similarly if your preferred way of cloning your dahlias is via cuttings, either in springtime from the tuber shoots, or during the season using lateral shoots from actively growing plants, then it is advantageous for your seedlings to strike easily and grow well that way. This trait can be genetic.

• Seed production:
The quality and quantity of seed produced will vary. Commonly, open centred dahlias will give a lot of seed but will more than often produce seedlings with an open centre.
Fully petalled doubles tend to give less seed, but depending on the pollen parent and which genes are passed on, the resulting seedlings tend to inherit a higher petal count as well.
Both quality and quantity can vary genetically, so best to observe and keep records if seed production is a trait you are wanting to breed for.

Some of these things may be self-assessing eg if you only propagate for subsequent seasons via tuber division, then a new seedling cultivar that does not make many tubers and is a poor storer, will likely die off over a few years without a lot of work, and won't tend to get spread around as easily as one that makes many robust tubers.

But as always, regardless of what you plan to do, observing, taking notes and keeping records will allow you to make informed choices.

Rooted cutting growing in pot

Keeping Records

As you observe the traits of your new dahlia seedlings, I highly recommend taking notes and keeping detailed records throughout the process, as it is surprising how much you can forget between blooms, and especially between seasons.

Start by keeping track of which bloom your seed comes from with labels on seed packets and tags in your seedling trays. As you start to catalogue the seedlings you'd like to keep,   make sure you tag them in a way that will last through the season, and then transfer that information to the tubers, and cross reference with your photos and notes. I like numbers, some people prefer working names.

Try a few methods or systems to find what works for you, The recording can be such a delightful part of growing and getting to know your own new dahlia seedlings.

To inspire you to discover your own method, here are some ways I've found are easy to keep my seedling records, and a few helpful tricks I've learned along the way.

Above, Recording details about seedlings - clockwise from top left: front/profile photos, relative size, "family portrait" photos and photos of multiple blooms from same seedling

Photos and Cataloguing

These days when most of us carry a camera in our pocket in the form of our mobile phone, it can be very simple to keep a visual record of your blooms, captioned with an identifying name or number.

On my phone, I just swipe up on the photo in the basic App photo gallery, and the metadata is revealed and type in a caption. For simplicity, my caption is a single identifying code which has 2 digits for the year then 3 digits for the unique number of that seedling and then an abbreviated seed parent name (and pollen parent if known)
So for example, in 2024 I started a lot of seed collected from open pollinated 'Devon Salmon' seed, and one of the catalogue numbers was 24-589DS. The photos instantly give me quite a lot of information about the seedling. Visually I see the colour and form, the catalogue number indicates which season it was started and seed parent, and metadata photo date tells me date of first bloom.

Moreover, it is quick and easy to do a search for that catalogue number in my gallery and I instantly see all the photos of that bloom that I captioned through the season, which gives such a great overview. (See right)

The same catalogue number will be written on flagging tape that is tied around the base of the plant, and is also listed in my field notes.

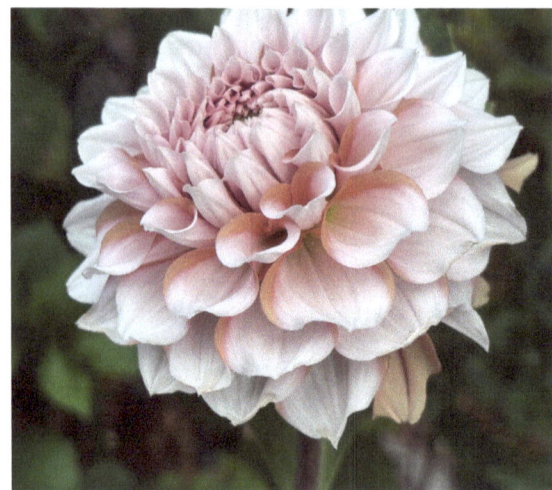

Seedling #24-589DS Photos taken throughout the season to track changes

I make sure to take photos across the season, and am careful to take them in good light (but not direct sun) which generally gives the most accurate colour. I'll make a note if I can't get the colour in the photo quite true to life so that in winter when I have more time to look through everything and make some more decisions, I don't get thrown by the colours being different to reality.

I also make sure I take a photo of the front of the bloom so I can see the relative petal size/shape/arrangement, and from an angle that best shows the overall form of the bloom. I take a side-on profile photo that will remind me at what position the head was sitting on the stem. This can definitely change through the season, so it is great to compare those profile images as the season progresses.

If later in the season a plant gives a good flush of blooms at the same time (or in second, third, or subsequent seasons when you may have multiple plants), it is also useful to see a handful or bucketful of all the same seedlings together in a photo, as it shows the range of variation and you can often get a more complete view of the form of the blooms when seeing multiple flowers together.

At right: 'Serenade Nereda' record keeping photos.
Top - front view with hand for scale
centre - profile view for head angle
bottom - multiple blooms and stem

Comparison photos of various seed parent with related seedlings

The other photos I like to take when I can, are side-by-side comparison photos of the seedling next to the seed parent (see images to the left).

Where I have quite a few seedlings from the same seed parent that I plan to keep, it can be very helpful to see them all laid out together and sometimes a loose impression of common traits can be gained by doing this. You can intuitively learn quite a bit about genetic inheritance by doing this.

If the bloom colour or petal shape is unusual I might also take photos of individual petals next to the full bloom so that I can accurately remember more about what made the form or colour significant.

You can then keep a folder of images on your computer, or add them to a spreadsheet program like AirTable, If you are more tactile you can print out the best couple of each seedling and make cards or scrapbook them into your field note book if you have one.

Bloom with unusual colour petals

This page: sibling seedlings

Field Notes

Having accurate photos can make a lot of field notes redundant, as you can instantly see so many of the bloom characteristics at a glance, and visually observe nuance of form, petal shape etc that would take a lot of describing to explain and still not always capture accurately. However, I still learn a lot from making myself categorise and describe what I am observing, so I take the time to take regular notes at least on my top contenders.

Grab a notebook and pen, or make notes on your phone (I simply use the 'notes' App on my phone to type a few observations about each seedling) or, if you are able to set yourself up with a spreadsheet or similar record-keeping system that you can access on your mobile as you are working through the plants that can be a great way to keep everything together easily too.

I love the idea of an old-school visual scrapbook with printed out photos or polaroids of your seedlings along with detailed field notes, lovingly rendered watercolour or pencil sketches in a botanical style, or a dog-eared notebook with grubby fingerprints where descriptions and details have been scribbled down hastily out in the garden.

However, my own record keeping has ended up all digital just because it's quick, easy and functional.

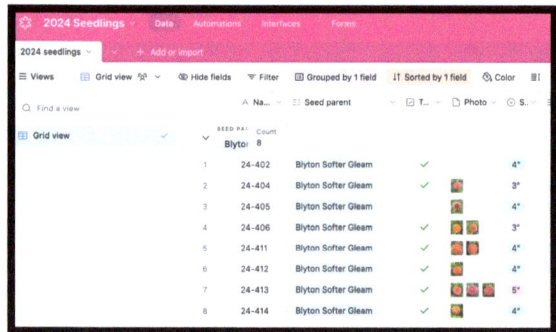
Screenshot of my AirTable file on laptop

I like AirTable which is an online spreadsheet file platform. I can have the mobile App version out in the field with me, which then automatically updates the version on my computer when I want to refer to details back indoors or during winter as I plan out my next season planting.

I also like it because you can have photos in the same file as your notes which saves multiple references and opening back and forth between different files. It also streamlines what notes I keep, as I don't necessarily need to describe colour and form changes over the season, when I can see those things in a single glance at a well lit, well-angled photo.

You might not need to keep any notes about the colour if you have a photo that is true, but if you are using a spreadsheet program and at some point you would like to filter your records for example to see all the "peach" seedlings that you have tagged to keep, then it is useful to allocate each seedling to a colour group, or other category that you set up.

Also, one thing a photo won't necessarily give you is an indication of size, unless you have some objective measure in there. I used to take a photo of each bloom next to my hand for scale, but a ruler or tape measure, or standard show sizing rings are more precise if you want to keep a visual record. Instead I now take note of size in my field notes (via dropdown list in my AirTable), since I've no need to be precise, but this allows me to filter by size when needed.

Because of my specific breeding goals, I will always critically assess and take notes on the stem strength and suitability for cut flowers, how robust the attachment, and what the position is like, and also petal count and how it holds its centre as it opens completely. Generally unless there is something unique about the bloom that makes me curious enough to explore breeding it with a stronger cut flower or to pursue just for interests sake, I'll remove the seedling at some point through the season if it doesn't pass on those four criteria. The acronym I use to make sure I'm always assessing and recording this is SAPC. I ensure that for every bloom I check Stem, Attachment, Position, (petal) Count. Again, I have each of these criteria in my AirTable field notes. Other traits like the petal shape or form are obvious from the photos I have taken, but I do make notes if there is anything particular about the bloom that isn't immediately obvious from the photos I've added.

Beyond this, I will note outstanding traits, like a very healthy plant, a particular tall or compact plant, or if I notice it to be especially floriferous. If a plant has a lot that I like about it but something is not ideal, I'll make a note eg to check the head position later in the season, so each time I go back in to add notes I'll see that and it will remind me to observe if that is a consistent problem, or it was just in the first flush.

It's useful from start of season to make a list of traits you'd like to record, but still leave room for extra notes, and it's likely you'll find your own personalised system will evolve after doing it for a few years. I find that some traits that are essential for me (such as having self-supporting plants that don't sprawl all over the place) I don't need to include a note on this in my field notes, since I am really tough on that trait when I'm deciding whether to keep to remove a seedling, and I'll rarely keep one that annoys me like that - if it's persistently horizontal after giving it a bit of help initially, it's straight to the compost heap. On the very rare occasion that the bloom is just too appealing to dismiss, I can always make a note in my "additional notes" field to keep an eye on it for sprawling in the second season. Occasionally when grown from tuber and in a more optimal position in its second year, it can prove itself to be strong enough to grow without supports, but more often than not, if it doesn't improve, I'd prefer to just be rid of it earlier than later.

Above and At right: photos of various seedlings for my records

Here are categories in my field notes for first year seedlings in may AirTable files. This is very specific to my breeding goals, so you need to add your own criteria. It is also likely that even by next season I'll be tweaking this layout and adding and subtracting fields to make it even more useful to my record keeping.

DIGITAL FIELD NOTES

Name: *(code number eg 24-589DS later changed to working or release name)*

Current: *(a yes/no toggle that I can turn off if I cull the plant later)*

Photo: (I upload & manage photos to the file here)

Photo comments: open descriptive text field where I comment if the colour is not true in the photo (eg darker than looks, cooler pink, more golden), and anything about the form that might not be obvious from the images

Size: (dropdown menu - 3", 3.5", 4", 5", 6"+ although we work in metric in Australia, I find inches easier to estimate)

Stem strength: (drop down menu - excellent, great, ok, fail)

Attachment: (drop down menu - excellent, ok, check future blooms, fail)

Head position: (open text field so I can comment multiple times through season, common notes are "perfect 45", "check future blooms", "clock faced first bloom")

Petal Count: (dropdown menu : VHigh, High, Medium, Low)

Plant health & vigour: (descriptive text field)

Additional notes: (descriptive text field)

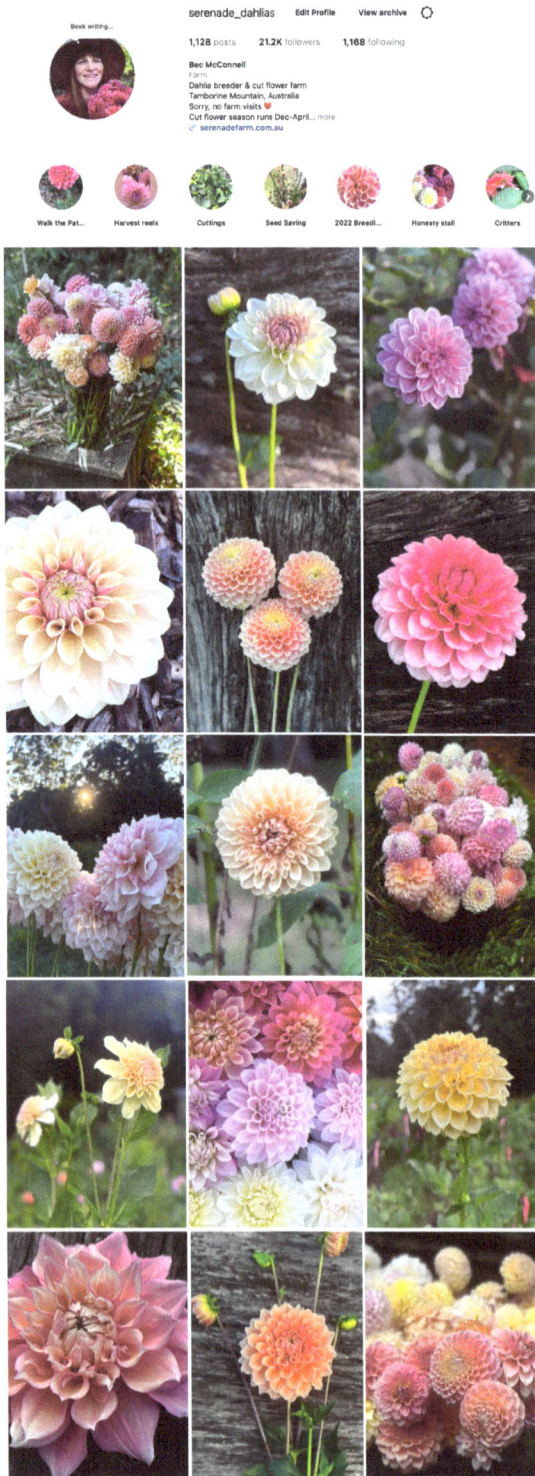

Part of my less conventional, and also less systematic, record keeping is by posting almost daily to my Instagram feed online during the season.

My posts often reflect upon new seedlings, or the reasons behind why I plan to keep or remove certain ones, including their strengths and weaknesses, or anything unusual I've noticed as I observe them.

What I like about doing this, in addition to taking that time each day to photograph and comment about a specific seedling, is that followers sometimes highlight features or issues or traits that might not have at first been obvious to me. It also encourages me to explain and justify why I would be exploring a certain seedling line, or in some cases dropping some that don't fulfil my goals. I need to ensure I don't let external perspectives affect my decision making too much, as photos only show a limited amount of information about a seedling, but I do enjoy stretching my perceptions a little, and having the opportunity to see how certain seedlings are perceived from the outside, and even what the current trends and fashions in dahlias are in different places too.

Author's @serenade_dahlias Instagram profile

Record keeping for show growers can be very systematic, and as we've discussed there is already an excellent list of criteria on which to measure your dahlias.

If you grade your blooms in the same way that they would be judged in the show, then the consistently highest scoring blooms would be both worth keeping and hybridising from in future to create your own quality breeding lines.

Knowing the seed parent (and preferably also pollen parent if exclusively hand pollinating for your seed) will give you clues to which dahlias are best for you to continue hybridising with in future. We'll be talking about line breeding, with back crosses and sibling crosses in the chapter on intentional hybridisation, but without effective records a lot of that is purely guesswork, and not particularly efficient.

Creative Approaches to Dahlia Observation

Not everyone is a spreadsheet or details person. If you don't feel inclined to be assessing your new dahlia seedlings to exhibition criteria or with scientific precision and grading them according to petal curvature or measurements, or head angles in degrees and ratios of width to height, it doesn't mean you can't become your own expert of your new dahlia seedlings. There are so many creative ways to get to know them, to explore details you might not otherwise notice in ways that can be more relevant to you personally. And in the process, you not only benefit by enriching your appreciation for your dahlias, but might have a lot of fun!

The suggestions over the next few pages are not specific to blooms that you have grown from seed, but our seedlings can often give us quirks and unusual features that lend themselves to creative expression even more than commonly available named cultivars that you grow from tuber or commercial plants.

Below: unnamed seedling from Red Rabbit Blooms

Florist

This is perhaps the most obvious way to engage with your dahlias. Cut & arrange in a vessel, play with different colour palettes and also learn how long they last in the vase, and how they respond to different styling approaches. You'll discover nuance to their colour and which tones blend well with others, and which textures give variation within a large group. Spending time with the blooms, handling them, observing them in a relaxed way, comparing them to other blooms in the arrangement, all can give insight into their strengths and weaknesses.

Through this creative but also practical approach you can discover both the functional and aesthetic qualities of your unique dahlias.

Photographer

Both in the field, and in the studio, take time to style a photoshoot with your new dahlias and photograph from various angles. Process images to really explore the shapes and forms and how different they can appear in different lights and from different angles. You don't need to be a professional photographer to benefit from exploring your dahlias through photography, and likewise you don't need expensive equipment or studio lights and backdrops to do this. Even using your phone camera and taking time to find a natural or neutral backdrop, and preferably looking for soft, diffuse or reflected light that will give true colours. Avoid harsh shadows or bleaching out the colours caused by direct suns. Like many dahlia growers, my camera roll is 99% photos of flowers, it's something that has become integral to my enjoyment of the cultivation process. I derive so much pleasure from capturing them in various stages before the blooms fade.

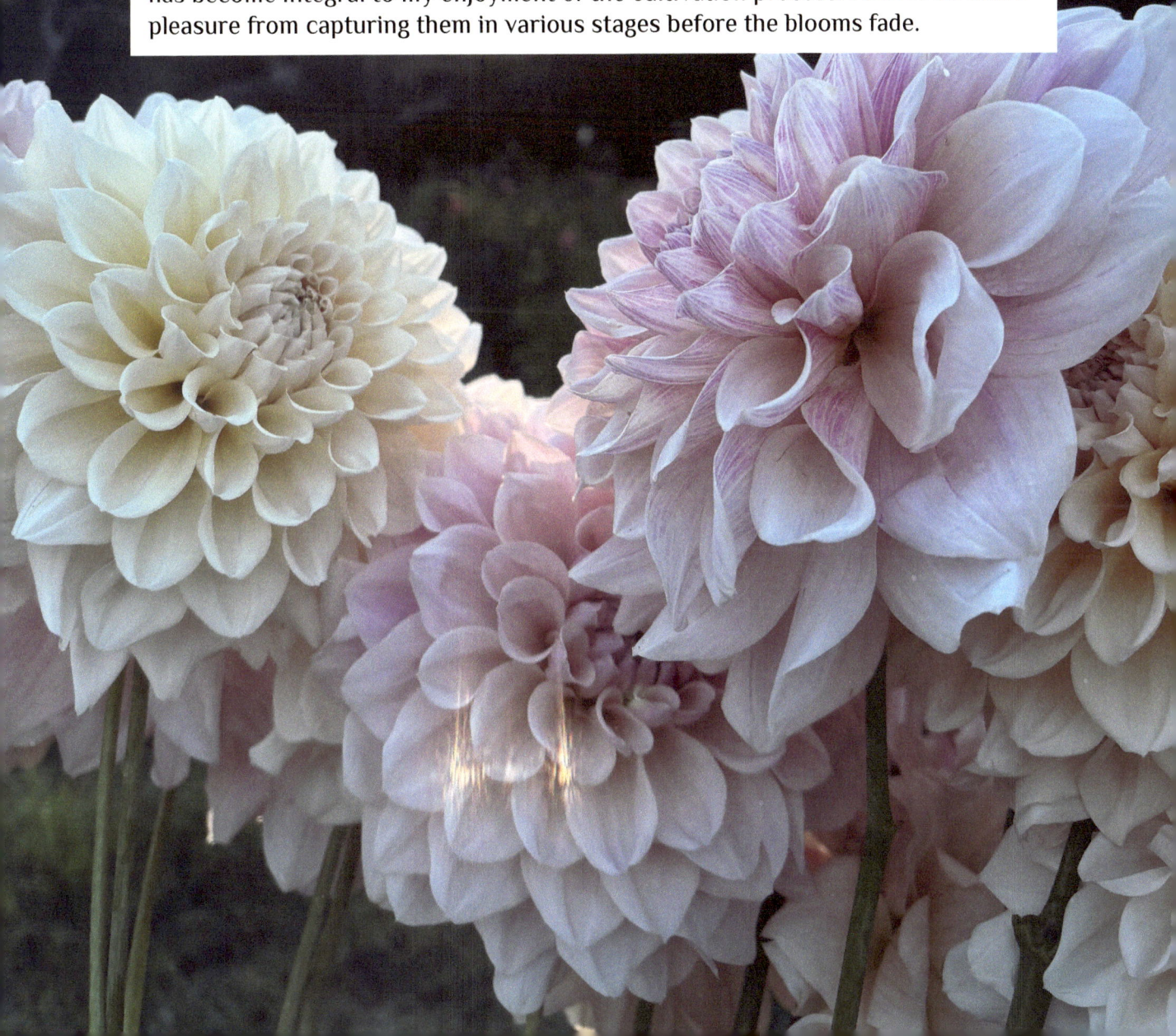

Writer

Describe your blooms in detail. Although on face value this may sound like your field notes, (and there can be crossovers here), but if you have a gift for language and enjoy writing, your field notes don't need to be objective, dry and scientific.

Describe in a more metaphorical way, or invent new terms for those in-between forms that we discussed, finding associations or how a certain bloom might bring up memories or inspire you creatively in some way.

I challenge you to wax poetic on your newest dahlia crush. Why not even a creative poem or haiku?

Artist

Sketch, paint, embroider or craft your seedlings to learn more about each bloom's form, colours and unique characteristics. When we recreate an image of our blooms we need to really look at them in detail - to capture their essence and what makes that dahlia special.

I learned about paper crafting when an artist asked permission to recreate my 'Serenade Curiosity' seedling after I posted photos to instagram. What she produced was a phenomenal likeness, and not only demonstrated incredible crafting skill, but exceptional observation skills, having never seen it in real life (she was in Europe, and my bloom only exists here in my garden in Australia.)

I have a friend who paints her dahlias and through her eyes and skilful brushstrokes, I can see so much extra detail and nuance in the way the petals curl, and heads hang.

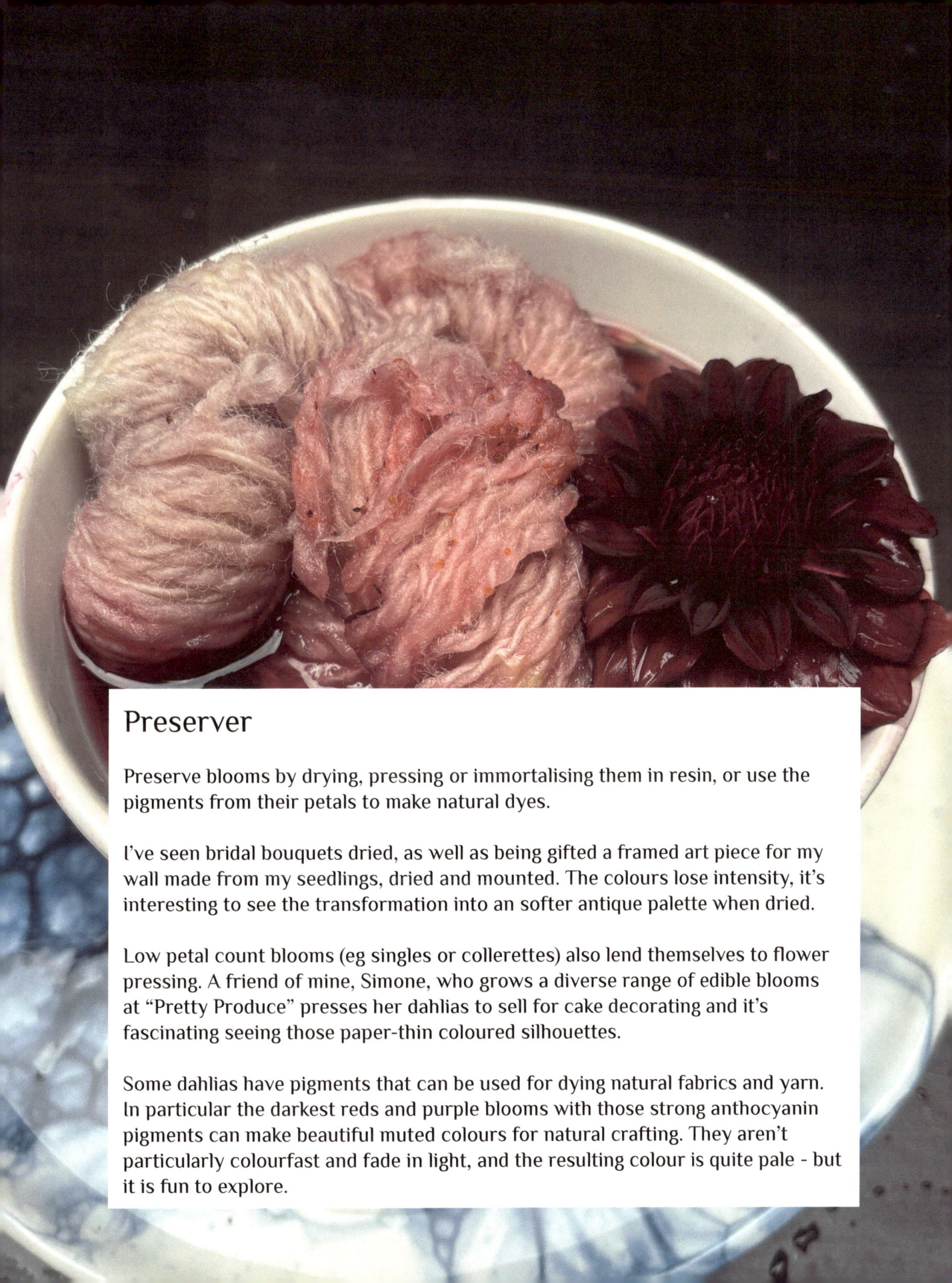

Preserver

Preserve blooms by drying, pressing or immortalising them in resin, or use the pigments from their petals to make natural dyes.

I've seen bridal bouquets dried, as well as being gifted a framed art piece for my wall made from my seedlings, dried and mounted. The colours lose intensity, it's interesting to see the transformation into an softer antique palette when dried.

Low petal count blooms (eg singles or collerettes) also lend themselves to flower pressing. A friend of mine, Simone, who grows a diverse range of edible blooms at "Pretty Produce" presses her dahlias to sell for cake decorating and it's fascinating seeing those paper-thin coloured silhouettes.

Some dahlias have pigments that can be used for dying natural fabrics and yarn. In particular the darkest reds and purple blooms with those strong anthocyanin pigments can make beautiful muted colours for natural crafting. They aren't particularly colourfast and fade in light, and the resulting colour is quite pale - but it is fun to explore.

Musician

Perhaps this is a stretch, but as a musician I couldn't possibly ignore the creative art of music, so why not if you have the skillset, compose a piece of music that is inspired by a specific dahlia, or the way that it makes you feel? The idea of these creative approaches is to look at your new seedlings with curiosity and an inquiring mind. Even without true synaesthesia, certain colours might link with sounds or at least feelings. I haven't done this myself yet, but as a musician and sometime-composer, I think I might have to put this challenge on my list for next season!

The author playing her Harp. Photo by Alison Roberts

Botanist

I learn so much more about my dahlias by carefully dissecting and pulling apart my blooms. You don't need to know the names of the flower parts (although any basic botany book can teach you those if you are interested) It's interesting to see how different blooms compare and how a flower is built from all its components. I love observing how these transform as the bloom moves from bud to blossom, opens to reveal the pollen and then matures into a ripe pod with seeds. I love playing with petals.

Foodie

Since dahlia blooms are edible (and in fact have been found to contain polyphenols that can be beneficial to our health!), Go to town in the kitchen, decorating cakes and desserts with petals or whole blooms, or add a sprinkle of petals to salads or as garnish to a meal. Speckled or ombré petals are a particularly visual addition to your food.

I was astounded to discover that there was a whole world of cake decorating that didn't use the blooms but instead recreated them in buttercream - the detail can be amazing. I have no doubt it takes a lot to develop that skill, but if that's your jam, then try recreating features you see in your new seedlings in your buttercream creations.

Mindful Meditator

Step out of the hustle bustle of life and just spend time gazing at your dahlias. With those visually pleasing natural fractals, meditating and contemplating your blooms not only allows you to be fully present in the moment, but can give insights about your seedlings that you might not have noticed otherwise.
You may like to arrange dahlia heads in simple shapes or Mandala patterns as a mindfulness practice focused on the beautiful colours and forms of your dahlia seedlings.

Intentional Hybridisation

Growing dahlias from seed is unpredictable - but the great news is that we can strategise to stack the odds in our favour to lean into our goals.

Not all dahlia seed is created equal. It is true that outcomes are highly variable, and even if you cross two known cultivars you can still get dramatically different offspring, even from the same seed pod. However, the genetic code embedded in each seed is built with half of the genes from the seed parent and half from the pollen parent. So if both parents do show strong traits that you are hoping to see in your new seedlings, you will certainly increase your chances.

Saving your own seed is the best way to guide this and optimise your chances for results that are pleasing to you. You will need to start by making some educated guesses at what combinations may generate good odds for the outcomes you want. When you start, I highly recommend you pursue multiple approaches and then observe and record your results and refine things the next season.

Let's explore ways to hybridise and cross the best parents to align with our goals.

Breeding Goals - Setting your Intention for Seed

We've already touched on having goals when we discussed assessing our seedlings. But there is another time when it is good to keep your destination in mind, and that's when you are planning your next season's seed.

Many gardeners who experiment with seed-grown dahlias start out just giving it a go and collecting (or buying) whatever seed they can find. Results can vary with this approach, even with clear assessment criteria.

Having a clear goal will give criteria for assessment, but moreso it can help inform the types and colours that you collect seed from. You do need to make some good guesses, as a lot of genetic traits will be hidden, so even basic record keeping, by noting down the best seed parents, can help refine your results each season.

Another thing to keep in mind is that breeding a stable cultivar that fulfils your initial concept isn't always the final destination. There is so much to be learned and discovered along the way, and it can be just as satisfying to get utterly distracted in the process and pivot on your goals midway through and take another unexpected tangent that excites you.

Without a doubt, my primary reason for growing from seed is to learn. To indulge in pure unbridled curiosity and delight. I do have a number of specific "ideal dahlias" that I am working toward, but it is the weirdos and peculiarities that always catch my attention and make me wonder where it might lead if I pick up those threads of curiosity and follow those down unimagined dahlia rabbit holes of wonder. However, I sometimes need to take those delightful weirdos and intentionally cross them with other reliable cultivars that have the functional qualities that I also require in my dahlias.

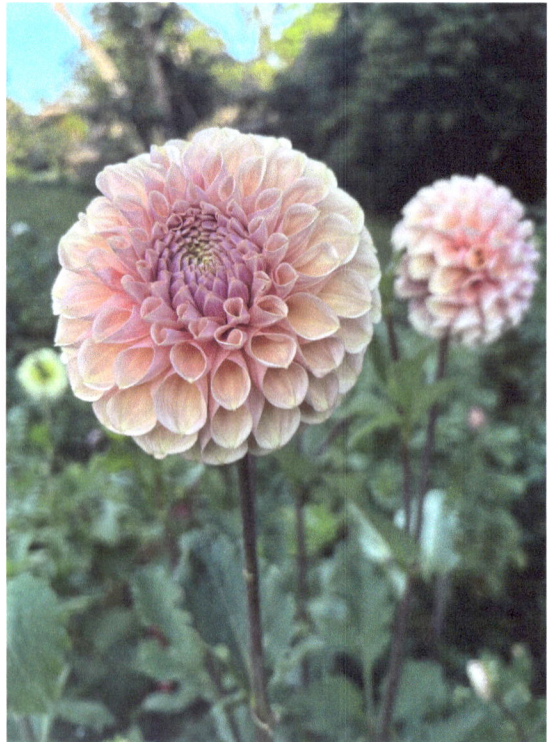

One of my seedlings on the way to a perfect pastel bouquet dahlia, with exceptional functional traits

Here are a few ideas you might like to pursue as you plan how to implement the strategies in the next few pages.

• Breeding for genetically fresh Exhibition stock. Spend time at exhibitions and society field days and get to know the cultivars that most commonly win in each class. Get a copy of the standards and judgement criteria to form the foundation of your assessment. Choose a type, acquire some excellent examples to grow and use some of the intentional hybridisation techniques we're about to discuss in this chapter. You may even find a mentor at your society who can guide you in your journey and help towards your goals.

• Breeding for commercial cut flowers. The functional traits like stem strength, head attachment and position, ease of care, floriferousness, vase life, and colours that suit current floral trends tend to be non-negotiable, so you'll be looking for those traits in both your seed and pollen parents.

• Breeding for the unique, unusual and quirky. Be a courageous adventurer and expand on the fashionable or typical forms, colours or readily available cultivars. This goal may begin by being more experimental, and involve crossing diverse forms and colours and then selecting anything that is particularly eye catching. However, I will add, just because a seedling is unique, that is not necessarily enough to give it value. How is it different? And is that a forward evolution or a backward one? Often

a new unusual seedling will just be one step in the journey, especially if alongside the eye catching difference, it carries faults that need to be addressed, such as inconsistency, lack of vigour, malformed blooms, poor health.

• Breeding for a specific bloom colour or colour combination/pattern, or even foliage colour.

• Breeding for a specific form or petal shape

• Breeding for plant height (especially tall, or dwarf plants that don't require staking)

• Breeding for specific bloom size

• Breeding for health, vigour, pest/disease resistance, tuber formation and storage

• Breeding for local climate suitability, especially if you are growing in a marginal climate where dahlias typically struggle - you can select for the ones that thrive (or at least survive!) in your conditions.

• Breeding for early flowering types, or late flowering types related to day length triggers, or plants that sustain well giving a steady flow of flowers all throughout the season.

• Breeding for the next dahlia "unicorn".

Pollination Strategies

The simplest option to produce your own dahlia seed is to let nature take its course. Leave the plants to bloom to maturity, allow insects to pollinate at their discretion, then when seed forms on the plants simply collect that once mature.

This is known as **OPEN POLLINATION**. Even with no knowledge or control over where the pollen comes from, this can still give delightful results, particularly if you're not fussy about what seedlings you grow the following season.

If you grow any open-centred dahlias they do tend to dominate simply because they open quickly, have a lot of pollen available, and the insects will spread that around very readily. Open-centred genetics can quickly become prolific in your genetic pool even if you only collect seed from the fully double plants. Another thing to note is that some colours also tend to proliferate a bit - genetic instruction for yellow pigments come through quite frequently, as do strong dark reds. However, there is still a lot of variation when the genetics mix, and again it depends on the exact cultivars as to how much weight their genetic code gives to those colours - a reminder that there is no simple dominant/recessive code like diploid humans have with eye colour.

However, there are easy ways to take some control over which cultivars are contributing their genes to your seed even when allowing insects to pollinate. Which strategy, and the degree to which you control the variables, depends on the amount of time you have to invest. You can either just make small tweaks or you can implement multiple consistent strategies to optimise your outcomes. There are no guarantees, and generally you can't be certain which cultivar contributed the pollen.

Implementing any strategies to limit which cultivars are available to pollinators is known as **SELECTIVE or CONTROLLED OPEN POLLINATION** In this case you are still allowing the bees and insects to do what they do so very well, which optimises the pollination process, but you reduce the options, and so are hacking the process to some degree (without the bother of time-consuming hand pollination.)

Remember, nothing is certain, but there is a simple principle with dahlia breeding that you can follow - "like with like gives (a better chance for) like". So as an example, a bright pink crossed with another bright pink gives a better chance at getting more bright pinks than if you cross a white with a yellow. Or a giant crossed with another giant will give you a better chance of a bigger bloom than if you were to cross two smaller cultivars. And if you stay curious and observe and keep records, you may be able to refine that further when you discover common results from specific cultivars.

'Serenade Whisper' (above left) with eight results of controlled open pollination seedlings above right

Controlling by Cutting Back

The simplest form of selective open pollination is to grow whatever dahlias you like wherever and whenever you like, but to cut back anything that you don't want to contribute to your gene pool at the time of pollination. This can be a deep, hard cut back of all stems (taking a third to half of the plant away - especially any budding laterals), or if you are diligent and are in your garden every day, and still want to see blooms on those plants at some point before the season ends, this can be disbudding any and all buds that are colouring up on the plant. With the latter approach if you have open centred blooms (singles, collerettes etc) you do have to stay on top of this, as the blooms can move from coloured bud to open bloom with accessible pollen very quickly.

Then after removing all buds, whatever is left blooming will be the combination that your seed may contain. In a smaller garden with small number of cultivars it can be much easier to limit the options for the bees in regard to the style, form, colours that you prefer.

Seedling obtained from selective open pollinated seed

Controlling by Curation

Choose and limit dahlia cultivars that you grow to match your goals. If you are trying to get only orange dahlia seedlings, only grow orange dahlias in your garden. It still definitely won't guarantee only orange seedlings, but it is going to better your chances for orange offspring than if you grow a large range of colours.

Similarly, if you are hoping for tightly formed ball types of dahlias to come through in your seed, only grow those types in your garden so that the chances that the pollen half of the genetics will also be from a ball type when you collect your seed from a ball.

Anecdotally, breeders have reported that using white dahlias in a form/type you are trying to breed from will give a good diverse range of colours that are more likely to be of that form. It's not always true of course, and some white dahlias will pass on their form more strongly in their genetic code than others, but you could try that if you are breeding for form, and remember to keep records of the seed parents that you collect from to refine that in future seasons.

Peach coloured seedlings

Controlling by Garden Design

Since dahlias experience a period of winter dormancy, we have the perfect opportunity between seasons to plan the way we will layout our plants in the next season to assist the pollinators to combine preferred cultivars together.

For example, if you would like to breed for specific colours but don't mind what form the dahlias are, then you can simply design your layout in blocks of colours. Plant all the whites together, all the burgundies together etc. The amount of nuance in this planning depends on how specific your goals are. If you want a high degree of control, this is where detailed observation of your potential seed and pollen parents can make a difference, as you will notice that dahlias typically express a range within these traits. So thinking of colour not only in big classification "bins" of "White", "Pink", "Orange" but planting the cultivars in a gradual shift of colour from clean white to warm white to lemon to yellow to apricot to peach to pink will potentially further optimise the outcomes. And colour isn't the only spectrum to consider in this way. Petal shape, and petal curvature, and form, and all the other traits we discussed can be considered in the planting plan so that bees are more likely to combine the most similar cultivars together.

Even without strict layouts, I've had a lot of success by designing my farm in "hubs" - loosely grouping my seed parents based on certain traits I was hoping to breed for.

The best example of this you can see on the page opposite. I created my "petaloid hub" where I carefully planted only seedlings and cultivars that had petaloids (or I had noticed that as a seed parent in previous seasons had produced seedlings with petaloids).
I allowed only those blooms in that area to open their centres and set seeds in early Autumn, carefully cutting back any other blooms nearby, and harvested and recorded the seed parent.

The following season I had dozens of petaloid seedlings result from that seed. Since it is a trait that has been selected against in the past for exhibition breeding, typically petaloids are not all that common, but in a few short years my patch is filled with them!

"Petaloid Hub" Seed Parents

A small sample of resulting seedlings with petaloids

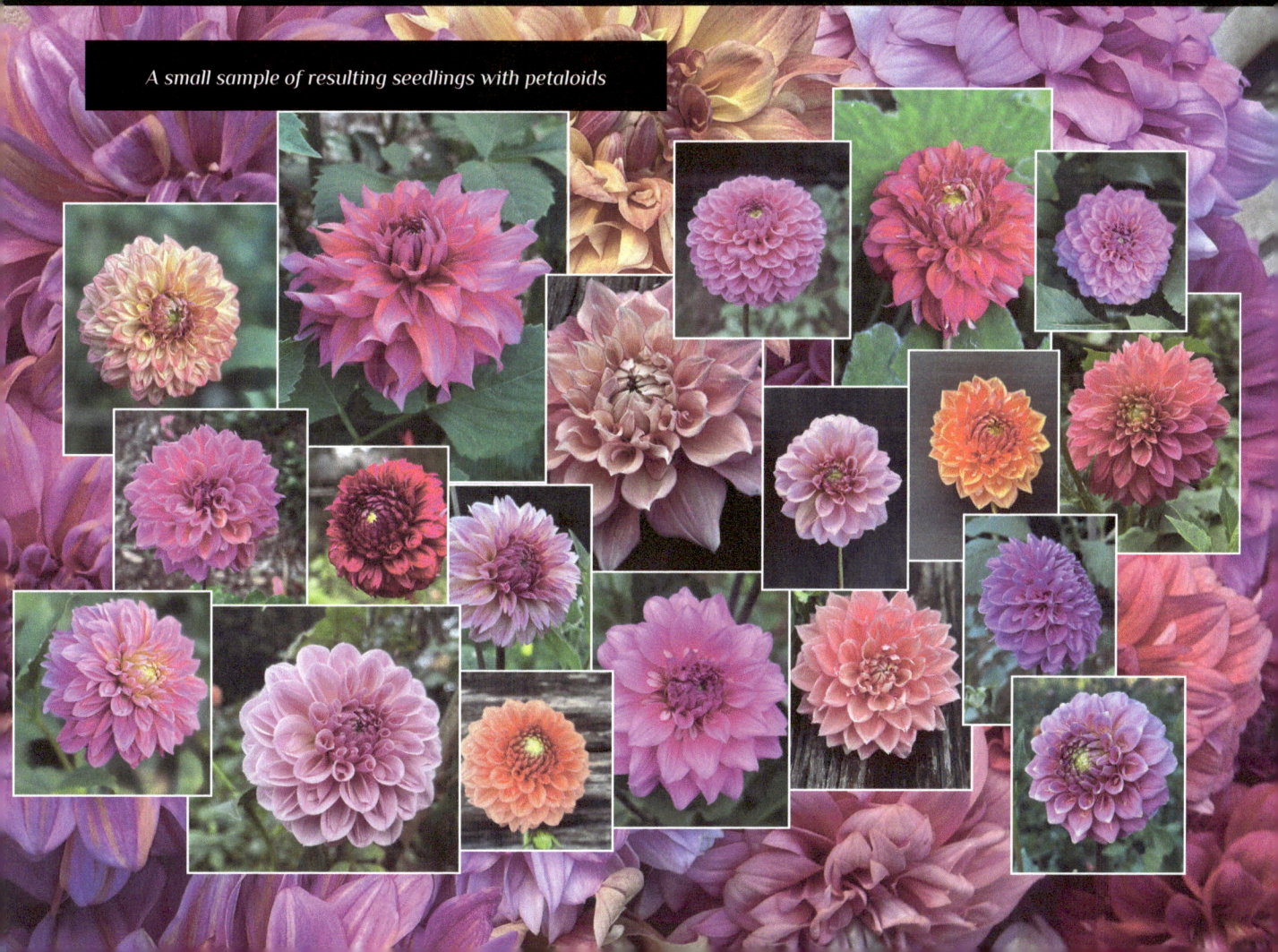

Controlling by Separation
Isolating by Space or Time

Taking the previous strategy a step further, if you would like to still grow a diverse range of forms or colours and don't want to limit your garden to only those that meet your breeding criteria, you can still manage the pollination by taking into account physical structures around your growing space, or timelines of pollination.

You can have an isolated garden bed somewhere further from the rest of your dahlias. Ideally if they can be separated by a physical barrier such as a building or solid structure, hedges/dense trees etc this will be a more effective strategy. It won't completely eliminate the possibility that insects will pick up pollen from other dahlias before they visit this area, but they do tend to fly along in straight-ish lines, so once they start moving from flower to flower you are increasing your chances. Creating "Bee Highways" (named such because bees do tend to move along a row of plants quite systematically) is a commonly used strategy. You can even rig up temporary structures such as shade cloth between rows to "herd" your pollinators in the right direction.

Greenhouses or shade houses or other contained growing spaces are another excellent way to physically separate your chosen cultivars - just remember to ensure that pollinators still have good access to these spaces.

Better still, if you have a friend or family member who is happy for you to plant a bed of dahlias on their land completely isolated from other dahlias this can be the perfect way to keep them separate.

Unnamed Serenade seedling under assessment

Alternatively, use **time** as your separator instead.

I like to grow and collect seed from some open centred dahlias, in particular, scented collerette blooms. If I tried to do this at the same time as my other open pollination, I would struggle to get a high petal count on all my other full doubles.

However, I simply do this earlier in the season (late Summer), allowing them to pollinate and set seed and collect this early, and then cut back those plants low, and don't allow them to flower at all whilst the pollination of the rest of my plants is happening.

This page and inset: Collerette seedlings

Growing Seed or Parent Plants in Pots

If you have a seed parent that you want to collect seed from and would like to give the best chance of certain pollen being deposited on those blooms (without hand pollinating), you can grow that cultivar in a pot (that you are still able to lift and move around when it gets to full height). When this cultivar blooms move the pot to be in the middle of a block of plants that you would like it to be crossed with. Ideally if you have plenty of plants the pot can be completely surrounded by the preferred blooms and the chances of it being pollinated by those is very high.

The other advantage with this is that if you are experiencing a very wet autumn, you can place the pot out in the garden to be pollinated on sunny days when pollinator activity is high and pollen is dry and viable. Then if you get some very rainy days in the subsequent weeks, you can shift the pot under cover to protect the maturing seed pod from staying wet and the risk of rotting.

Similarly a pollen parent can be introduced in a pot to a specific location to direct pollinators to introduce that pollen to a block of seed parents.

Vases

A similar strategy can work (only for pollen parent) if you don't have the cultivar growing in a pot. Cut a mature bloom which has opened sufficiently and place it in a vase/bottle of water nearby the preferred seed parent plants. The cut flower won't be suitable to produce any seed, but it will continue to open further and produce more pollen for several days sitting in water. If the weather is cool and fine enough, this might be ok to be left outside, but you risk losing pollen to insects. Alternatively keep the blooms in a vase indoors and bring it out for a few hours each day at peek pollination time (when you see lots of bees around)

Pegs and Ties

If your preferred cultivars are growing close enough to each other but there are a lot of other dahlia plants nearby, you can improve your odds by carefully pulling stems across from nearby rows and using a clothes peg, twine or zip tie to bring the stems close together, so the open blooms at a compatible stage are directly next to one another, and increase the chances of insect pollination between those two blooms. It is necessary for the blooms to be at the right point with the pollen parent producing pollen and the seed parent with stigmas available, but if that timing aligns then the pollinators can help you hybridise your preferred cultivars together.

At left:
By placing 'Serenade Curiosity' in a pot within a block of 'Sugartown Sunrise' plants (pictured), I successfully bred four different seedlings that based on their appearance quite possibly were fertilised with Sugartown Sunrise pollen.
Insets show 'Serenade Curiosity' with her seedlings

Hand Pollination

If you have the time and inclination there is so much to be gained by controlling with certainty both halves of the genetic potential of your seed by selecting and recording both the seed parent and pollen parent.

EXCLUSIVE HAND POLLINATION is the way to do this. First, select which cultivar will be your seed parent, and which your pollen parent and look for buds starting to colour up. Cover buds on both plants before they open with a barrier to prevent insects introducing random pollen into the bloom (organza bags are effective). Then when blooms reach full maturity and both the pollen and the stigma (tiny yellow 'Y" shaped structures) are visible, temporarily uncover and carefully brush or rub pollen collected from your chosen pollen parent onto the stigma, and then recover. Repeat for several days as more pollen is produced and more stigma mature. Ideally this should be done when the conditions are dry and warm. Bees present around other blooms is an excellent sign. Wet pollen won't be viable, so if you have a lot of rain then it won't be successful.

Common practices to collect and apply pollen include using a fine paintbrush to remove the pollen from a mature bloom into a clean envelope or similar, and then immediately brushing it over the stigma of the chosen seed parent. Alternatively collected pollen can even be stored for a couple of days, or potentially for longer in the fridge/freezer (but either way ensure that it stays completely dry) if your intended seed parent is not receptive to pollen when you harvest it. It is possible to collect the pollen from mature blooms that have been cut off the plant and kept in a vase indoors. They can continue to produce pollen for several days.

Cut blooms with lots of fluffy pollen can be VERY GENTLY rubbed over the top of a seed parent bloom, so that the pollen is deposited directly onto the stigmas. Cover seed parent back up and return the pollen parent to a vase of water or discard. Repeat the process either with the same pollen parent bloom or another mature bloom from that same cultivar.

After several days of adding viable pollen to the seed parent bloom, you may notice that the flower starts to lose the back petals. For blooms that are still very densely petalled, (or in weather that has been a bit damp or humid), you can ever so gently aid that process. The reproductive parts of the bloom tend to draw inwards, and what was a very bright yellow starts to dull to a brown. Keep the flower covered as the centre disc starts closing up and then remove the cover when the pod has formed. Leave the pod on the plant until mature. (4-6weeks if possible).

The benefits of collecting pollen and hand pollination are clear - you choose with certainty which two cultivars you are hybridising. You also gain the potential to store pollen to hybridise cultivars that aren't typically flowering at the same time (early flowering cultivars with late, or giants that tend to be less floriferous).

Additionally, the knowledge you gain by observing multiple plants from that same intentional cross can inform you much more about commonly inherited traits than only knowing the seed parent and at best being able to just make a guess as to the pollen parent.

However, don't be discouraged if you get few if any seeds from your hand pollination attempts at first. Pollinating insects are very effective at what they do, and conditions do have to be optimal for full fertilisation to take place.

Sometimes as a backup I do HYBRID OPEN/HAND POLLINATION where I bring in specific pollen from my preferred pollen parent, but do allow insects to also access the bloom. There is absolutely no certainty to which pollen contributed to each seed, but it is another way to increase the odds of having your preferred genetics at play.

Proposed pollen parent + seed parent

In-Breeding

If you develop the skills of hand pollination, and you keep clear records of the parents, you can continue to control and refine the genetics in future generations of seed by intentionally hybridising your seedlings backwards ("back-crossing), or across with other "sibling" seedlings that were produced from the same original parent crossing (side crossing). By doing this you can potentially concentrate desirable traits, and reinforce qualities that you are hoping to discover in your seedlings.

If you have a new seedling that has demonstrated a really interesting and unusual trait that you would like to explore more, there are a couple of ways to attempt to do this.

Backcrossing:
1. Cross the new seedling with its SEED parent (if known), and grow out all seed to select for anything similar but better.
2. Cross the new seedling with its POLLEN parent (if known), and grow out all seed to select for anything similar but better.

Side Crossing:
3. Cross the new seedling with any other seedling that shares the same parentage (i.e. any other seedling with both the same seed and pollen parent) to select for anything similar but better.

Repeat crossing (this is NOT inbreeding unless you then go on to cross the resulting seedlings with the original seedling in a sibling cross):
4. Hybridise the same two cultivars (the seed parent and pollen parent of your new seedling) in the hope that similar but better combination of genes may be inherited in the next cross.

By continuing to select for your desired traits and repeating this process with the strongest, healthiest offspring from any of this hybridisation (any promising results from 1-4 above), you can potentially build up a lot more copies of the genes that you are wanting to see expressed in your own lines.

However, it is important to note that excessive in-breeding in any species, even genetically complex dahlias, can lead to loss of vigour, weak stems, poor health and tuber viability. The loss of genetic diversity that is the result of narrowing that genetic pool, can make them less adaptable to stressors. There is still no guarantee that the good traits that you were trying to concentrate will get inherited anyway - we are back to trying to strategise the best we can in the genetic lottery.

The term "healthy hybrid vigour" (or outcrossing, which is the opposite to inbreeding) comes from crossing genetically diverse cultivars. If you use line breeding strategies and start noticing the health of your lines starting to deteriorate it may be time to find an outside, unrelated cultivar that is healthy and strong but somewhat aligns to your goals, to re-invigorate the genes before continuing with this strategy.

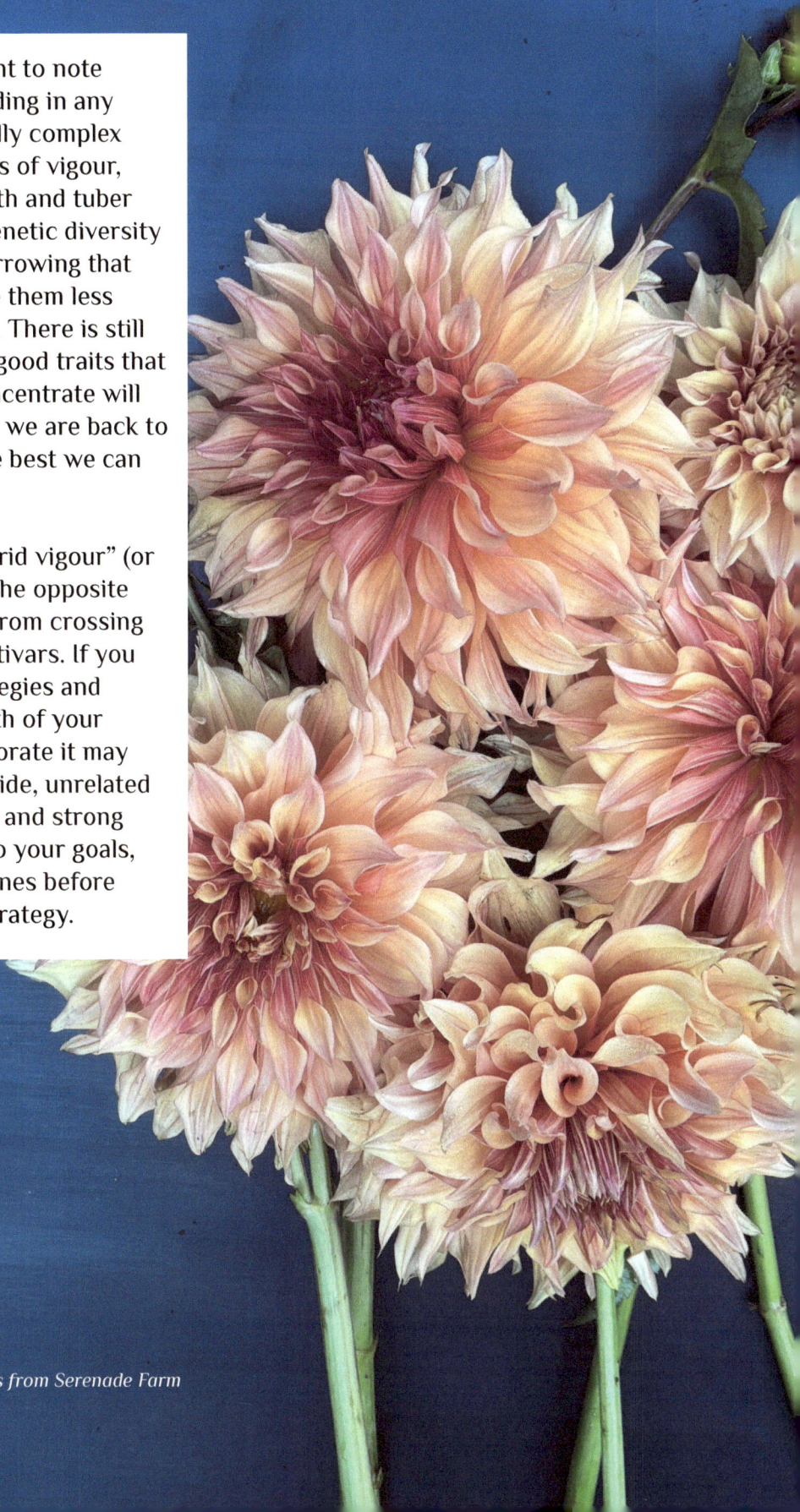

Both pages - unnamed seedlings from Serenade Farm

Timelines
for Dahlia
Breeding

They say patience is a virtue. When it comes to dedicated dahlia breeding, this is absolutely true. The good news is, you can derive enjoyment from the unfolding of the process, and learn so much along the way. The drive toward achieving a specific goal is only part of the picture, and it's not necessarily a matter of dull tireless patience if you approach it from that perspective. Gardening is well known for nurturing the quality of patience, as we have to think ahead, plan, mitigate, and hope for the best. There is an inherent optimism in planting a seed, and it does take time, so whether we like it or not, there is waiting involved.

Unlike more genetically predictable seeds, dahlias can sometimes be a large investment of time for little reward, as more often than not, we find that after months of nurturing, our new dahlia plants bloom and most are nothing like we were hoping. Bobble heads, weak stems, low petal count or hard centres, or colours that we dislike, are par for the course. But sometimes if we just make the experience an opportunity for learning, or allow our natural curiosity to take over and explore what we do find when the buds open, then it was not wasted time, but instead an experience that we can move forward from.

As the next season rolls around, we use what we have discovered and refine our plans for the future. Using the pollination strategies or trying hand pollination skills to more closely control the parentage of the following season's seed gives us the potential to move closer to our goals. Then the waiting begins again, for the next plants to bloom, and hope the results might be closer or more to our liking. It's a long game we are playing, so we may as well enjoy the journey.

Different breeders will have strategies that suit their particular situations and personalities best. Some will grow out huge numbers and hope for the best. Others will keep immaculate detailed records and do a lot of very intentional hand pollination, refining each season to get closer and closer. Some will have intuitive strategies, and have several concurrent approaches happening at once.

Particularly if we have a specific dahlia breeding goal in mind, and if breeding to share our dahlias with the world, it's important not to be too hasty to share or sell stock of our new seedlings. Take time to really explore, assess and get to know each new cultivar that arises from seed-grown dahlias.

We may be exceptionally fortunate, if stars align, to find a seedling in our first year that ticks all the boxes and fulfils a goal we were hoping for. However, it is still important to continue to assess that seedling over a number of seasons, to ensure genetic stability and also see how it performs under various stressors that may change from year to year.

Ideally we want to work towards evolving the whole dahlia genus to a stronger, healthier one. With this in mind, any stock that is sickly or not robust is best not to be spread around or sold.

I certainly support the idea that beauty is in the eye of the beholder, and is subjective, but when sharing and selling clones of my seedlings, I am contributing to the stock of cultivars that become available for future breeding, so I want to ensure I am improving the quality of the dahlia genus in a way that is meaningful to me at least.

I commonly hear the idea that one should assess their seedlings for 3 years before they release them. However, I've found that for me this would be a bare minimum. We are very fortunate here in our subtropical location to have a lovely long season. Depending on the plant, I can get dozens of blooms from a single first year seedling and have plenty of time and different conditions to assess the bloom. Even with this long assessment period, my first year really only gives me a limited snapshot of what the bloom is capable of, since it is a single plant. I'm more likely to make excuses for blooms that I love aesthetically even if they don't fulfil my functional criteria. There are certain faults (for me, most often to do with stem strength, attachment and position) that unless they pass (or have something truly exceptional about them), I will drop from my collection, and I do try to

limit myself to no more than 10% of the number I planted to keep on for further assessment.

During the second season I typically grow between 1-5 plants of each, from the divided tubers, and in a different location with much better supports in place and give them the opportunity to really prove themselves. I again try to cut the number right back in this second year to no more than 10-20% (which becomes more difficult because the reasons are more nuanced the second time around).

Then in the third year my selected seedlings become the backbone of my commercial cutting patch, and they have to prove themselves as a good productive cultivar that day in, day out, can be cut and included in florist orders. It is not uncommon for something I thought would be excellent to either show faults I hadn't noticed in the second year, or in some cases to deteriorate genetically in this third year (most notably to throw single blooms all of a sudden), or just not hold up well or give enough flowers to be viable to grow for my farm purposes.

At this point, (or even sometimes after second year if I have plenty of stock), I might send a few tubers or cutting-grown plants to experienced growers who have cut flower farms in different climates to trial for me and give me some feedback on how they find they compare to other named cultivars that they grow.

After the third year there might be the option to then share or release, but then it also depends on the amount of stock l have developed by this time. All going well, l try to grow 30 or so plants in the third year, so even if it is a good tuber producer, that doesn't give a lot to release if doing tuber division alone.

My preference, for a few reasons, is to sell cutting-grown plants rather than dormant tubers, which gives me the potential to propagate up a decent number of plants from those tubers to sell in late Spring. However, if a seedling is good enough for me to grow in very large numbers for cut flowers, taking a fourth or fifth year to grow more plants to cut from, and then release in larger numbers is potentially a better business decision for me.

Beyond this process of breeding specifically for my cut flowers, there are always a few seedlings that l will keep either for my own breeding lines, or as a personal indulgence because l just love them, even though they aren't ever going to be one of my main patch cut flowers.

Naming Your Dahlias

After investing all that time and energy into growing from seed, assessing and learning about your new seedlings and deciding you have a new cultivar worth keeping, when and how do you name your new dahlia?

Given that every single dahlia seed will create a new cultivar, when you grow a dahlia you like from seed you can give it a unique name. Other than going down the route of trademarking or registering Plant Breeder's Rights, in Australia there is currently no legal way to "register" a dahlia name.

In general, you can name your dahlia anything you like, as long as you aren't infringing on anyone's legal rights with trademarks. Some notable silly names I've heard include "Second Chook Shed", "Blah blah blah", "Spoiled Rotten" but it is more common for dahlias to be named after either people who are special to the breeder, or something that the dahlia reminds the breeder of, either because of the colour or some other association.

Often a breeder or dahlia enthusiast will use a specific prefix to identify it as one of their introductions. Sometimes this might elude to the location of where it was bred (eg "Bracken" dahlias were bred in Bracken Ridge, Brisbane, Australia), or a farm/property/business name (eg I use "Serenade" as my prefix, for Serenade Farm) or the breeder's name, family or initials (eg KA's for Kristine Albrecht's dahlia introductions, or Glenmarc named for Alf Hardingham's two sons).

If breeders choose to have a line of releases for different purposes (eg exhibition vs garden cultivars) they will maintain two different prefixes to delineate the difference.

In terms of when to name them - again this is up to you. Some breeders will name their blooms early on in the process, as they find it easier to remember names than catalogue numbers, others like to wait a few seasons to ensure that they will be consistent and continue to fulfil their breeding criteria in order to be worth naming. Some people are superstitious or don't want to jinx a new seedling by naming it too early, so they hold off until they are certain that it has passed enough seasons of assessment.

There may common practices or society guidelines in certain countries, but there are no overarching rules to naming your dahlias.

'Serenade Gaia' named for the author's niece who was born at the time the first bud of this seedling opened (above) and 'Serenade Citrus Twist' (below)

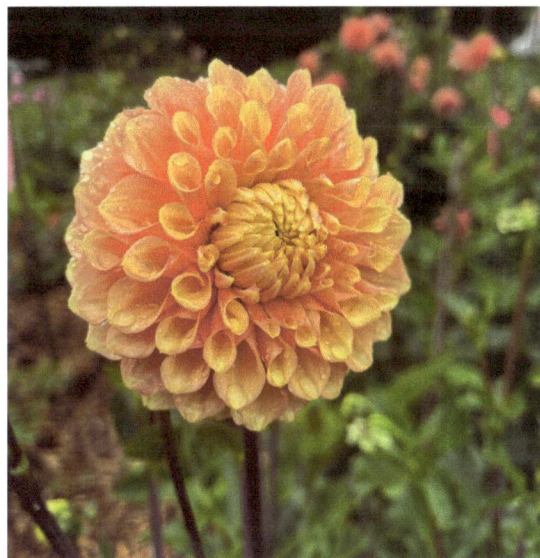

Propagation of Clones

Although somewhat tangential to the focus of this book, I find developing the skills to successfully propagate via cloning to be such an asset when you have grown a dahlia from seed and have assessed it and decided you would like to keep it long term, to ensure you don't lose that precious genetic material.

You may want to secure first year seedlings in case tubers fail or unexpected events (cows, floods, fires), or to build up stock quite quickly, or to have plants or pot tubers to share with others.

The methods of propagation that create an identical clone include:

Tuber division in Winter/Spring

A clump is divided into multiple sections which are replanted. There are many books, videos and workshops on tuber clump division that you can look up, as it is probably the most common way that dahlias are grown, and one of the more conventional and popular ways of cloning your stock. Splitting a dormant tuber clump, which you have dug up at the end of the season will guarantee an identical genetic copy.

Vegetative cuttings

Cutting material can be taken from a few different places on a dahlia plant.
• Tuber sprouts (first shoots from divided tuber, clump or pot tuber),
• Basal shoots (secondary shoots emerge from under the soil from the tuber clump after the main plant has started to grow),
• Stem sections from a growing plant (either lateral shoots emerging between stem/leaf, or alternatively from the growing tip of the plant but before primary bud forms)

Material for a stem cutting ideally should have 2-3 nodes - one at the base of the cutting, and one sitting above the surface of the medium. The roots will form from the lowest node and new growth from the top. All but the topmost leaves are removed, to reduce transpiration and moisture loss.

Tuber cutting bed producing multiple shoots perfect for taking cuttings in Spring

Plant material being prepared for cuttings

At Left: 'Serenade Fairylights'

139

Cutting material:
Top left - tip cutting taken from young plant in Spring. This section has then been trimmed to just below the node, and then the two lowest leaves will be removed.

Above - half-node cutting set into mix. New shoot will emerge from between half stem and leaf, and roots will form just below surface

Left - lateral shoot between stem and mature leaf, This shoot will be removed and trimmed down for cutting material.

Bottom left - half node cuttings (sometimes also called "leaf cuttings") where the stem is trimmed 1cm above and below the node and then carefully cut in half.

Another method involves further dissection of the plant material into smaller sections, with 1cm stem above and below the node, and then slicing this in half. Both the roots and the new growth will emerge from the leaf axil (junction between leaf and stem).

Regardless of the method used, once the cutting strikes and new roots are formed, the plant will develop and grow and be an identical genetic copy of the plant from which it came.

Dahlias grow quite readily from cuttings, and particularly the spring shoots from tubers are very receptive to this process. Success typically lies in finding the right balance in your conditions:

• Temperature: Keep the root zone at around 17-21 Celsius (62-70f), and don't allow the mix to go over 25c. Keep the tops of the cuttings cooler than this so that they don't need to transpire.

• Humidity: For the first weeks, place under a humidity dome or with very regular misting. Rapid dehydration due to water loss through the leaves will stress the cuttings to the point of wilt.

• Air/moisture Balance of the mix: Due to the soft fleshy nature of the material we use for dahlia cuttings, it is essential that the mix is not too wet. With no roots in the early stage they don't draw up that moisture. Use a very light airy mix - I make a blend with at least 50% perlite to maintain good aeration.

• Light: Remembering from our discussion on photoperiodism, more than 12hrs day length will help initiate root development. I set my full spectrum grow lights to 14-16hrs when first striking my cuttings to facilitate best feeder root development.

• Hygiene: Keep everything sterile to avoid spreading bacteria, fungus or virus between plants

Troubleshooting:
If your cuttings wilt or blacken you need to reconsider your temperature, humidity or moisture levels as it is likely something is sub-optimal.

If cuttings seem healthy but fail to show any sign of roots after 2-3 weeks, check to make sure they are getting enough light, if they stall at the callous stage they may not be getting sufficient light to trigger root development.

Half node cutting with developed root system 6weeks after taking cutting

Tissue culture
This is a sterile lab process using a very small segment of the meristem growing tip which is initiated into tiny plantlets and grown on to become a full sized plant. If grown in normal conditions for a full season it will also form a full tuber clump. Tissue culture method is generally used for large scale commercial production. Costs to initiate each cultivar can be quite high, so usually you would be looking to propagate many thousand plants at a minimum. It is usually done by contracting someone with a lab to do this for you, although home labs are possible.

Less common, but good to be aware of, are cultural practises through the growing season that can increase the number of tubers that develop. Each node, or leaf axil, has the potential to produce roots and therefore tubers. If you cover nodes on the stem or branches with soil and the temperature and moisture levels are right, new roots and tubers can form, given enough time and if the rest of the plant is actively growing and exposed to adequate light for those processes.

Simple ways to do this include:

Ground layering
Carefully lean a flexible branch over onto the ground without snapping it from the plant and bury a node or two underground. New roots and tubers can form from that point while the stem above continues to grow and potentially even flower.

Planting Deep
As mentioned in the earlier section on growing from seed, when transplanting either a seedling or rooted cutting, dig a deep hole or even place the plant on an angle, to cover up as many nodes as possible, (don't worry, the new growth will straighten itself up). If you do lean it sideways, remember to mark where you planted the original root ball for locating the main tuber clump at digging time otherwise you may damage this.

Mounding around the stem.
Don't be afraid as your plant gets taller to strip lower leaves and mound soil and mulch up around the base of the plant. Although with some other plants this would encourage rot, in dahlias this isn't a problem. Not only will this provide your plant with a lot more stability, but if you can mound up over a node or two you have the potential for new roots to develop from those nodes and even tubers to form too, given enough time.

Left and below: Serenade seedlings

Community

Dahlias are so inherently generous, with months and months of blooms, a big dividable tuber clump at the end of the season, and then the chance for seeds as well!. You'll find no end of dahlia loving friends happy to help take those bouquets, tubers and seeds off your hands!

Despite hearing murmurings of breeders keeping secrets in the past and not wanting to disclose any information about good seed or pollen parents, (and perhaps fair enough in the society competition environment, and I'm sure all in good fun and competitive spirit!), I have found dahlia growers and hybridisers to be extraordinarily generous with sharing information, time and even plant material with one another.

Left: 'Serenade Fairylights' and below, harvest of seedlings from Serenade farm

Dahlia Societies & In-person Connection

The buzz around a dahlia society or gardening club event is something else. When you gather people together in one place who share a common passion, the excitement and energy generated by connection with like minds is electric! Attending my first national dahlia conference, I was delighted to find that regardless of age, background or reasons for growing dahlias, there was a synergy through shared interest that generated such positive forward motion, and I would be surprised if not a single person came away without some new inspiration and fingers itching to get back into their dahlia planning (despite being the middle of winter!)

Dahlia societies or garden clubs provide not only eduction, field days, workshops and information specific to your local climate, but often opportunities for mentoring which can be invaluable for new growers. Dahlia societies facilitate annual exhibitions and competitions, and for those interested in developing their skills in growing and showing their dahlias it is such a great way to learn. For those who are growing from seed to breed dahlias for exhibition, it also provides the opportunity to enter seedlings into that class and have them assessed with an experienced eye, and to be provided with feedback on the traits that conform to the society standards.

In addition to the exhibitions, in some countries there are society-run trial gardens where you can send your selected seedlings to be grown out and assessed independently, again providing experienced objective feedback on them. Particularly if you are interested in breeding dahlias that are suited to exhibition, this can be invaluable.

Societies also provide access to tubers, plants and seed, and you can share your excess with other growers through these groups too.

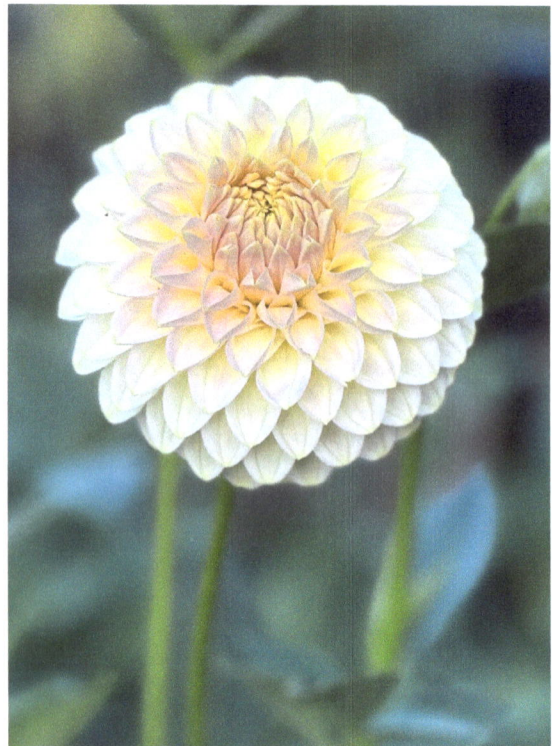

Above and at right: Serenade seedlings

Connecting and Swapping with Other Breeders and Growers

If you don't have access to a formal dahlia society, you may be able to initiate or find another way to connect in person with other dahlia growers nearby you. I know of small, informal, sometimes irregular, get-togethers of dahlia growers. Sometimes the focus is on micro-flower farming, or other times on gifting blooms for charity, open garden sharing or crop-swap type situations where tubers or seeds are exchanged, or just social visits to each others garden during the season to see and learn about new cultivars.

Growing dahlias from seed is such a vast landscape - and with the seemingly near-infinite genetic possibilities it can seem like an enormous task that we set ourselves when we first embark on a specific breeding goal.

When we think about where the modern dahlia has come from in such a relatively short period of time, we can be grateful to all those dedicated hybridisers who experimented and explored and shared what they found with others, and that generation after generation the dahlia was built into what we know today. Every time we collect a dahlia seed there is an ancestry that was influenced by those hybridisers from previous generations that we are tapping into.

Online

There are myriad reasons you may not be able to connect with other dahlia growers in person, and certainly these days there are so many ways to access information and support without doing so. Many generous, experienced growers and breeders will share a tremendous amount of helpful information online (zero cost) via their social media accounts through posts, videos and answering questions in specialised group pages. Where they provide the option, you can show your appreciation in tangible ways by subscribing to their channel or account, or buying their books or enrolling in online courses that some provide, where even more information is laid out in very clear systematic way. It's often the case with the courses there is ongoing support from those educators too.

Alternatively, valuing the way these growers have shared their experience, you can "pay it forward" in simple ways by helping out a new grower with information you found helpful, or giving a few dahlia seeds or tubers to a neighbour, or bunches of your beautiful blooms to a local aged care facility or other community organisation.

There are also several exceptional podcast channels that specialise either in dahlias, flower farming or backyard growing, and often experienced dahlia breeders and growers are interviewed on this platform and a wealth of knowledge can be obtained that way too. Electronic resources are constantly evolving, and there is a wealth of knowledge available on a multitude of platforms.

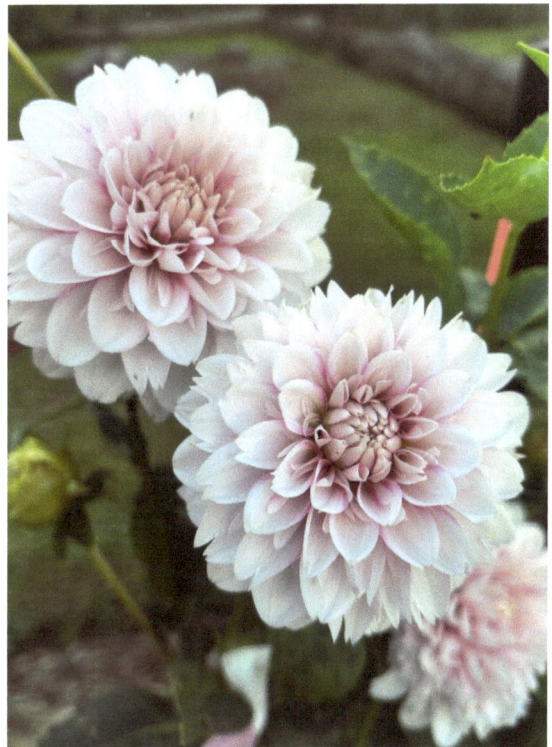

'Firetail CanCan' seedling sent to me by Ruth Downham from Firetail Gardens to assist with my petaloid breeding goals

When I discovered a little bloom in my first year of growing from seed that had multiple layers of petals and within each petal a tiny contrasting coloured petaloid, I shared photos online trying to understand more about this unusual form. The encouragement, support, suggestions and interest I received back was such a delight and certainly compounded my curiosity in this as one

'Oddity' a seedling that fuses anemone centre with several layers of petals with petaloids. Sent to me by Jill Hogan from Red Rabbit Blooms

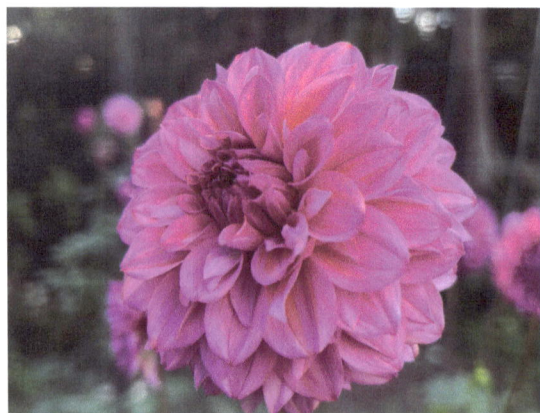

'Lileah Pink Petticoats' bred by Kate Mungoven of Lileah Dahlias, sent to me to assist with my breeding goal of fully double petaloid dahlias

of my future breeding goals (the goal crystallised into fully double blooms with contrasting petaloids that would function well as cut flowers). It also gave me a sense of responsibility as custodian to the unusual genetics that had come together in this bloom.

I got to work selecting and hybridising with this goal in mind (among others) and along the way I was contacted by a couple of other Australian dahlia breeders who had encountered blooms in their own lines that had petaloids. They offered to share these seedlings with me to further my efforts to this goal. Cutting-grown plants and tubers followed in the mail (since they live in different states, too far to visit). I reciprocated where I could from my own lines to support their breeding goals.

Thanks to setting up my little isolated "petaloid hub" on the farm (see p123 for visual), which only included petaloid seedlings (both my own and from these friends), in order to concentrate those genes for my selective open pollinated patch, the next season resulted in a tremendous explosion of seedlings with petaloids. Certainly my journey has been aided by the generous help of my breeding friends, the other advantage being that these additional seedlings had different seed and pollen parents to my own, ensuring plenty of genetic diversity for the healthiest most vigorous stock as well. It means that I have many seedlings to choose from and can select only the very best ones to move forward.

'Serenade Whisper' (left) and her seedling (right). I sent Serenade Whisper to be trialled in a couple of other gardens to see if her health issue persisted. It did, but fortunately it didn't get passed on to her seedlings

Trialling Your Seedlings in Other Climates

Another tremendous benefit in connecting with other experienced dahlia growers and breeders who live in different climates, is that you can do trades with one another of selected seedlings to trial in different conditions and get their feedback. (Subject to biosecurity laws of course.) This often reveals further strengths and weaknesses on how resilient or not they can be in hotter or colder or more humid or dry weather, and how they cope with being grown by a different gardener with their own style of doing things. Given that our climate here on Serenade Farm can be a bit humid and the days never get as long as they do in the southern states of Australia, I find that often my seedlings will in fact perform better for others than they do here (or maybe I'm just a hard marker!). I've found it effortless to find volunteers to grow out exciting new cultivars, and it's such a delight to get to reciprocate this as well.

Breeding Dahlias for Profit

If you aspire to develop a seedling to the point of releasing on a large scale for sale and profit, it is obviously important to first of all be confident that your seedling is genetically consistent and truthfully represented with whatever traits you present to market.

Images from various angles, or better still video, of the bloom in natural (but not over-bright washed-out) lighting that shows the colour faithfully and clear accurate information about size and characteristics such as stem strength or other traits not obvious from the photos.

Unless your plants have been virus tested in a lab it is not accurate to call them virus-free, even if you have not seen symptoms, but one would hope that you do have hygiene practices to minimise viral spread in your garden if you plan to release any cultivars for sale.

Because of the inherent ease of propagation once your have released your named cultivar to the public, it makes sense to maximise the number of tubers or plants that you sell in that first year of release. Many breeders will hold their new seedlings for at least 3-4years, but sometimes more, before the release to build up stocks by tuber division, but you can also augment the amount you have available to sell by propagating additional plants by vegetative cuttings, or if you have the capacity, even via tissue culture.

How many is enough tubers or plants to make a release viable? How long is a piece of string? I've heard various numbers thrown around from 30 to 100 to many more. Truly it depends on your objectives, your resources, and how you value and measure your time and resources that were invested in getting your cultivar to that point. Also, market demand will play a part in this decision too.

In some countries there are also farms running programs that can assist you to release extra special cultivars if you don't have the capacity to grow out enough stock yourself. Alternatively you may look at partnering privately with someone to do a similar thing, where royalties can be paid back to the breeder for the exclusive option to sell your new cultivar. Triple Wren Farm in the US have their "Legacy Program" which is a well established way they support small breeders to release new cultivars. Quite Contrary Flower Farm in Australia is starting up a similar program here too.

In the last few years, certain newly released cultivars, often given the coveted "unicorn" status, have been very high in demand and been priced accordingly and achieving very high selling prices in auctions and online sales. However, with the huge increase in the number of people trying to jump on this bandwagon and aspiring to breed the next "unicorn", it is likely that the market may be flooded with new release cultivars, sometimes of questionable quality, and this may have a follow-on effect of diluting the potential of the market of new releases. In particular, it may become more difficult for new breeders releasing cultivars that have not been tested or assessed by well known or independent growers to break into this market in any significant way.

Healthy Dopamine Levels

What is it about growing dahlias from seed that some of us find so addictive? Something I love with almost equal passion to dahlias (I did say almost) is learning about neuroscience and the way that the human brain works. One particular neuromodulator, dopamine, is responsible for goal setting, motivation and drive, and is a big player in the reward circuits in the brain. One thing that can lead to a healthy dopamine baseline is striving toward a goal that has unpredictable intermittent rewards.

I believe this is part of what makes growing dahlias from seed so delightfully addictive. If we have just enough information and resources to move toward a specific outcome, but there is still a randomness to the results, we have the potential for a burst of dopamine each time a bud opens and we get to assess the outcome. The concept is known as reward prediction error - and when we are putting in effort - leaning forward into something, this compounds the sense of satisfaction when we succeed. If we were either to succeed or to fail every time, however, we would tire of the process and no longer feel that motivation to move forward.

All this to say, that growing dahlias from seed might take time, and might take effort, and might not always give us the results we hope for. But despite these things, it can be intrinsically rewarding on a very biological level.

Growing dahlias from seed, particularly with specific goals in mind, and a plan to select and assess over a number of seasons is such a wonderful, healthy antidote to our instant gratification culture. I've personally also found it to be such a satisfying way to step outside the competitive consumerist model of trying to score the latest unicorn dahlia in online tuber sales.

Instead, the infinite possibilities from seed may result in untold unimaginable "unicorns" that will magically appear by collecting seed from your own beloved cultivars and rolling the dice with the near infinite permutations of dahlia genetics!

Some seedlings that might pop up with irredeemable (but sometimes still loveable) "faults" I may not grow more than a season or two, or if they do they'll just have a little spot in my own personal garden (and maybe if they are lucky a square on my instagram grid) and the rest of the world may never own one of them, regardless of how "magical" it may be. When I hear people bemoaning missing out on specific unicorn tubers on their wish lists, I always suggest they take up growing from seed. It may be a little less predictable, and take a little longer sometimes, but it certainly delivers such tremendous delight when that extra special seedling opens for the first time anywhere in the universe!

About the Author

Rebecca McConnell lives and grows with her husband, Jon, and their two pups, Scout & Daisy, on "Serenade Farm" on Tamborine Mountain in subtropical Australia.

Bec's personal story doesn't follow the typical flower farmer narrative of dreaming of always growing flowers as a little girl. Like many others, she did have exposure to gardening from her grandparents and her Dad, and certainly as she reached adulthood, something that was very integral to her sense of purpose was to grow and nurture plants, but at that time, that was specifically centred around food plants. When Jon & Bec married in the late 90s they travelled the UK working on organic farms, and upon returning to Australia they enrolled in horticulture courses to learn more, and planned to buy land to live a healthy and sustainable life growing food.

However, as often happens, life took twists and turns, and distractions came in the form of running an entertainment business for 20 years before they purchased a little piece of paradise on Tamborine Mountain. Their original vision did come to fruition and they became heavily involved in a local growers co-op, supplying organic veggie produce for a few years, including those couple of tumultuous covid-19 years when there was a very high demand for locally produced fresh food.

It was also during these years, that the flowers infiltrated the veggie patches.. Beginning with edibles and pollinator-friendly species, and then more often the dahlias were given the best areas, and took up more space. Bunches of fresh cut dahlias were sold on the roadside honesty cart (and still are) as well as through the local organic market. Dahlias were just so generous with their bountiful harvests, so desired by local customers, and had captured Bec's heart.

After growing from tubers for around 5 years, the first year that Bec trialled growing some of her own open pollinated dahlia seed, she grew out 350 seedlings and was astounded by the quality and variety of beautiful new blooms that resulted from them. Keeping around 100 that first year, she was perhaps over ambitious and under discerning, and only a few of these have since made it through the many additional years of assessment, as well as exceedingly wet seasons, plus a freak tornado one year and tropical cyclone the next.

One of the very first odd little seedlings to bloom in that first year of growing from seed was unlike anything she had seen before. Between the layers of peach toned petals were what she later learned were termed "petaloids". The bloom had an open centre and a very poor head attachment so was not useful for her cut flower orders, but her curiosity had been piqued and she certainly wasn't going to cull this unique little dahlia, which she later coined 'Serenade Curiosity". Amongst the seedlings she also observed petal shapes and colour combinations that were so different to what else was available, and without hesitation she took an enthusiastic leap down the wonder-filled rabbit hole of dahlia hybridisation

The next year, she collected much more seed and grew out over 2000 new seedlings, and since then, many thousand more...and the rest, as they say, is history.

Gratitude

There are so many amazing people who have supported my dahlia journey, and I am so grateful to you all.
I dedicate this book to you.

Thanks to my dahlia friends and mentors. To my hard working, inspiring flower farming buddies and the dahlia society elders all around Australia, and the many dahlia lovers I've met online.

I'm grateful to Kristine Albrecht who has freely shared so much knowledge both through her books and extensive public eduction as well as through our many private messages over the past few years and encouraged me in my own dahlia breeding endeavours.

Thank you to my dear social media followers on Instagram for your support, feedback, encouragement and endless messages.

I am eternally grateful to my beautiful friends, Alison Roberts, Ali Rodway & Geoffrey Badger, Annelie Westerlund, Mardi Rhoden and Jon Lintott who all helped by proof-reading the book, and made many gentle helpful suggestions.

Love to my Mum, for nurturing my creative soul and at the same time allowing me to be my down-to-earth practical self, and Dad for instilling a love of nature, and to both of them for originally seeding the idea of writing this book!

And to my soul mate and love, Jon, who claims to just do the "donkey work" around the farm, but whose key insights and thoughtful solutions inform so many aspects of my dahlia growing and breeding journey, not to mention every aspect of my life.

Further Reading for Dahlia Lovers

Albrecht, Kristine and Brion Sprinsock (2023) "DAHLIAS: Seed to Bloom: The Dahlia Grower's Companion"

Albrecht, Kristine with Brion Sprinsock (2020) "Dahlia Breeding for the Farmer-Florist and the Home Gardener: A Step by Step Guide to Hybridizing New Dahlia Varieties from Seed"

Benzakein, Erin with Jill Jorgensen and Julie Chai (2021) "Floret Farm's Discovering Dahlias: A Guide to Growing and Arranging Magnificent Blooms"

Menzel, John (2016) "Dahlias in Australia: The Winkie Way"

Rhoden, Mardi (2023) "Flower, Dig, Divide, Repeat: A Quite Contrary Dahlia Workbook"

www.ingramcontent.com/pod-product-compliance
Lightning Source LLC
Chambersburg PA
CBHW041548260326
41914CB00016B/1588